HAMMERIN' ROUND

ROUND

SPEEDWAY IN THE EAST END

West Ham, 1948. From left to right: Arthur Atkinson, Howdy Byford, Malcolm Craven, Bob Harrison, Tommy Croombs, Kid Curtis, Aub Lawson, Cliff Watson, Stan Greatrex and (on machine) Eric Chitty.

When a knight won his spurs in the stories of old,
He was gentle and brave; he was gallant and bold,
With a shield on his arm and an lance in his hand,
For God and for valour he rode through the land.

No charger have I and no sword at my side,
Yet still to adventure and battle I ride,
Though back into story-land giants have fled,
And the knights are no more and the dragons are dead.

Let faith be my shield and let joy be my steed,
'Gainst the dragons of anger the ogres of greed,
And let me set free with the sword of my youth,
From the castle of darkness, the power of the truth.

HAMMERIN' ROUND

SPEEDWAY IN THE EAST END

Brian Belton

First published 2002

PUBLISHED IN THE UNITED KINGDOM BY:

Tempus Publishing Ltd
The Mill, Brimscombe Port
Stroud, Gloucestershire GL5 2QG

PUBLISHED IN THE UNITED STATES OF AMERICA BY:

Tempus Publishing Inc.
2A Cumberland Street
Charleston, SC 29401

Tempus books are available in France and Germany
from the following addresses:

Tempus Publishing Group
21 Avenue de la République
37300 Joué-lès-Tours
FRANCE

Tempus Publishing Group
Hockheimer Strasse 59
D-99094 Erfurt
GERMANY

British Library Cataloguing in Publication Data.
A catalogue record for this book is available from the British Library.

ISBN 0 7524 2438 6

Typesetting and origination by Tempus Publishing.
PRINTED AND BOUND IN GREAT BRITAIN.

CONTENTS

ACKNOWLEDGEMENTS

My grandmother used to sell West Ham Speedway programmes. She once told me that the men who rode the bikes were the greatest sportsmen who ever lived. They would use body, mind and spirit to contest their races. Bravery, intelligence, and a high bodyweight/strength ratio was required. They needed to be competitive, but also be able to entertain. They succeeded in this dual task, to the extent that they drew people to watch them in their tens of thousands; men admired them, women loved them, children worshipped them – these were no mean men and they captured that most elusive of entities, the spirit of their time. This book is written in homage to those brave riders and particularly the men who wore the claret and blue, with crossed hammers on their chests.

What follows was only possible because of the great help, generously given, by the Speedway Veterans' Association. In particular, this history owes its existence to two former Hammers. One is a true giant of the sport (in every sense of the word) and a man who is part of the history of the oval tracks, Reg Fearman. The other is probably the most active historian of the side and speedway in general, Terry Stone. They both possess all the qualities of speedway riders, but they are also good and kind people, hospitable and humane. It is their devotion and love for this most romantic of sports that this work is dedicated to. It may be of interest to note that the quotations at the start of each chapter are taken from *The Speedway Annual*, which was co-edited by Peter Arnold, the announcer at West Ham Speedway for many years. 'Up the 'Ammers!'

Left: *Reg Fearman*. Right: *Aub Lawson, Aussie Hammer, 1947.*

FOREWORD

It was in 1946, when West Ham Speedway reopened after the Second World War, that I first saw the Hammers in action. My parents, who lived in Plaistow, just down the road from the home of West Ham Speedway, Custom House Stadium, had been life-long supporters of the team and the sport, having watched the first meetings at High Beech in 1928.

That introduction to West Ham Speedway, with the thrill of the riders broadsiding and the silver sand, which was the surface of the track, spraying in a plume behind them, the smell of the methanol and Castrol R oil burning in the racing engines and 40,000 fans screaming with excitement, gave me the desire, along with thousands of other kids, to emulate our heroes. For us kids, it all started on the cycle speedway tracks which mushroomed around the East End of London. West Ham Speedway was extremely popular on Tuesday nights. In 1946, I would go straight from school at 3.30 p.m. to take my place in the queue at the turnstiles to save a place for my parents and sister until 6.00 p.m. Then, along with other kids, I would run round to the back of the stadium and bunk in under the fence!

I was luckier than most. Cliff Watson, the Australian, came to stay with us for the season when West Ham signed him in 1947. A few weeks later, he asked if his friend, Aub Lawson, could also come and stay. They were with us for several seasons. Unbelievably and suddenly, at fourteen years of age, I was in an extremely privileged position with two Australian internationals sharing our terraced home in New City Road. The bobby-soxer fans of the day camped for hours outside our house for auto-graphs and a glimpse of their idols. At the end of the 1947 season, just before Aub and Cliff left for Australia, Aub obtained two 1928 Douglas machines on loan for me to practice on during the winter of 1947/48. He brought them home on a trailer and said 'Here you are, Junior, see how you get on with these'. That winter, I rode one machine or the other on the Beckton Cycle Speedway track, pushing it the two miles from home. In February 1948, I graduated to the West Ham small practice track in the car park of Custom House Stadium and from there to the silver sand race track.

The West Ham management – all pre-war England internationals – promoters Arthur Atkinson, Stan Greatrex and manager, Tiger Stevenson, had a good youth policy and gave us youngsters tremendous encouragement. In May 1948, my parents bought me one of Cliff Watson's modern racing machines for £150, which I rode at West Ham practice sessions on Wednesday mornings from 6.00 a.m. to 8.30 a.m., following the Tuesday night's race meetings. Aub and Cliff were always present at these practice sessions. The reason for the early start was that greyhound racing took place on Wednesday evening, and the tarpaulins protecting the greyhound track from the silver sand had to be lifted and the stadium made ready. After practice, I had to pedal my bicycle like fury up Prince Regent Lane to Balaam Street so that I wouldn't be late for school.

At the age of 15 years and 3 months, I took part in my first public race meeting at Rye House on 1 August 1948. It was an individual event – the Holiday Cup – and Wally Green, who was then riding for Hastings, presented the Cup; not to me, but almost. I

Left: *Ever a Hammer – Cliff Watson*. Right: *Aub Lawson, leg-trailing in 1947.*

scored 11 points out of 15 and fell when second. This prevented me from contesting a run-off with Dennis Gray of Wimbledon, who scored 13 points to win the meeting. The Auto Cycle Union and Speedway Control Board promptly banned me from racing in public, declaring that I was too young and that I should wait until I was sixteen.

So, on the evening of Tuesday 26 April 1949, West Ham captain Eric Chitty presented me with my racing licence in front of 40,000 Hammers fans – a tremendous thrill. Racing with West Ham at the other London speedways – such as Wimbledon, New Cross and Harringay – was incredibly competitive. Every team had its star international riders and at Wembley, in front of their regular 60,000 fans, it was simply awesome. It made one feel like a gladiator performing in the arena of Roman times. The West Ham riders had a terrific camaraderie and would discuss team tactics before each match. As individuals, Eric Chitty, Malcolm Craven and Aub Lawson were always capable of taking first prize in a Championship event. Eric Chitty was frequently called to the microphone during the interval of a match to sing to the fans. He had a good voice, Bing Crosby style, and cut several records in the late 1940s and early 1950s.

In fact, they were all charismatic men. Malcolm Craven often flew his own aeroplane to speedway meetings on the Continent and would arrive at West Ham in his 1946 American Buick convertible. Aub Lawson, known as Gentleman Aub, was a hard man on the track but an absolute gentleman with the crowd, and he would stand for hours signing autographs. As my mentor, he said to me at the beginning of my racing career 'Junior, when you go to a speedway meeting, make the crowd remember you – score a maximum or knock off their best rider.'

In October 1950, as one of the youngest selected, I sailed from Tilbury for Australia with the England team, captained by Jack Parker. We lost the series but the experience was invaluable. After National Service and eighteen months of racing in New Zealand, I followed in the footsteps of a number of former West Ham speedway riders, namely Bluey Wilkinson, Arthur Atkinson, Tiger Stevenson, Stan Greatrex and Aub Lawson, when, in 1960, I promoted my own speedway track in Stoke-on-Trent. A change of career saw me promoting for twenty-five years at a number of different venues throughout the country as well as in Egypt, Kuwait and the United Arab Emirates – but, regrettably, not at West Ham.

Throughout my life and wherever I have been in the world, West Ham Speedway has remained close to my heart, and I have always been ready to talk openly and affection-ately about my time with some of the greatest speedway riders of that era. Any rider who has pulled on a Hammers race jacket has always remained very proud to have done so. West Ham had champions in each decade – in the 1930s, these were Arthur Atkinson, World Champion Bluey Wilkinson and Tiger Stevenson; in the 1940s, Eric Chitty, Malcolm Craven and Aub Lawson; in the 1950s, Australian Jack Young (twice World Champion) and Wally Green; in the 1960s, Scotland's Ken McKinley, Norwegian Sverre Harrfeldt, Malcolm Simmons and, of course, former World Champion Tommy Price as manager. Team spirit was always a key word with the Hammers.

Much of my time since retiring from active speedway has been spent in contact with members of the British Veteran Speedway Riders' Association, of which there are over 600 members. There are similar associations operating in Australia and New Zealand.

West Ham car part practice track, January 1948. Reg Fearman (foreground) is on a 1928 Douglas and Alf Viccary rides a Martin JAP.

When West Ham Stadium was demolished for housing many years ago, thousands of former fans and riders had tears in their eyes. The speedway, however, will live for evermore, not only in the hearts and memories of people like myself but factually, as a number of the roads on the estate that now stands on the former site of Custom House Stadium are named after eminent former West Ham riders – Wilkinson, Atkinson, Croombs, Baxter, Young, Lawson and promoter Hoskins.

I know this book by Brian Belton will make armchair broadsiding compulsive reading.

To win without risk is to triumph without glory.
(Corneille, *The Cid*, 1636)

Reg Fearman
Former member of West Ham Speedway team
Former British Speedway Promoters Association chairman
England Speedway Test Team manager
England World Team Cup and World Pairs manager, Great Britain Speedway Test Team manager
England Speedway Test Match Rider, Veteran Speedway Riders' Association president, 1992

Left: *Aub Lawson and Reg Fearman being presented with the Senior and Junior Conran Trophies.* Right: *Travelling man, Eric Chitty. The West Ham team captain and a mechanic demonstrate how the professional racer got about before the Second World War.*

INTRODUCTION

The Starting Gate

Perhaps the main piece of specialist electrical equipment on a speedway track is the starting gate. When the referee flicks the switch to shut off the current, the heavy-duty elastic contracts and pulls the tape carrier up very quickly until it slams hard against the rubber buffer at a top of the mechanism. There are other designs, but this is the most common, the main alternative being a magnet operating the reverse way round, working a hook arrangement on the bottom of the tape carrier, the sudden surge of current pulling the hook out of its position and thus releasing the tapes. Some gates do use springs instead of elastic, but these are very rare. It is interesting to note that the innovation of the starting gate probably saved speedway racing from a premature death in the early 1930s, for it did away with the rolling start which was so unsatisfactory and was causing enormous discontent among the fans of those days.

Silver, L. 'Anatomy of a Speedway' in *The Speedway Annual* compiled by Silver, L. and Douglas, P. (London, Pelham Books, 1969)

A huge, buzzing crowd encircles the floodlit oval, a dirt band lit up in the East End night, illuminated, 400 metres in a theatre of speed. The tension grows as the time ticks towards the first race. At the pit gate, four dark knights adorned in leather sit astride their exhaust-smoked, revving chargers. Last adjustments to helmets and gauntlets are made, as much to placate nerves as anything else. Fuel switch on. Signal for a push start.

The bikes circle cautiously, bound for the starting tapes. The floodlights flicker across the riders' team emblems that bedeck their collective rainbow of race jackets. The starting marshall motions the bikes up to the tapes, the green light throws out its message, every eye homes in on the starting gate. The tapes fly up, like a huge, elongated, albino bat. Engines snarl in response, propelling the quartet of metal steeds into a hail of dirt and shale created by the madness of spinning rear wheels.

The four hurtle into the initial bend; the monstrous bikes lean sideways into surreal broadsides. The helmeted pilots are now involved in a fight to hold the mechanical hurricanes, but there is not a thought for giving quarter. Wheels are forced into a wavering approximation of equality as the contestants hammer down the back straight. Four laps are eaten, at an average speed of nearly fifty miles an hour. The war to out-race and out-think is compressed into something little more than a minute by a chequered flag. The smallest slice of a second can make a rider a champion or a loser, a somebody or a has-been. Every individual in the crowd has filled their eyes with the brief, uncomplicated, profound action. The whole moment has meaning created by a panoply of phenomena that ignite reality into the fantastic metallic metaphor that is speedway.

The East End Connection

This racing sport is just one form of motorised competition taking place on an oval circuit. The basic tenets of oval racing go back at least as far as the Roman chariot racing that took place in the Coliseum and across the Roman world. Speedway is one of a group of closely related 'oval contests', that include motorcycle racing on indoor ice ovals of little more than a hundred metres in length; stock cars moving at 200 mph on high banked super speedways – like the 2.66-mile Alabama International Motor Speedway in Talladega; sprint car confrontations in Sydney; ice action in Kazakhstan;the Indianapolis 500; freight trains at Daytona; power boating on the Danube or in Singapore harbour; and snowmobile shoot-outs on the frozen lakes of North America. From Alice Springs to Pocono and from Prague to Ulan Bator, enthusiasts of the oval trial gravitate to see the gladiators of internal combustion strain for victory.

As such, oval racing, of which speedway is a species, is nothing less than a global sport, geographically and technically speaking. Its collective spectator potential across the planet would rival any sport. However, this book will focus on West Ham Speedway and will, as such, be concerned with that genre of motorcycle competition. Nevertheless, it would be unrealistic to tell the tale of the Hammers without framing their existence within the wider context of the speedway, which includes its evolution and development up to and including the years when the East End's team gave way to time. So, this history will start from the birth of speedway and conclude in 1972. Thereafter, speedway without West Ham, but with the likes of Ivan Mauger and the Grand Prix, is another story, to be told at another time.

Motorcycle sport has relatively long roots in East London and West Essex (of which West Ham was a part until the early years of the twentieth century). For example, on 19 July 1903 an 'International Motor-Cycle Race' took place in Canning Town, at the Memorial Grounds, the former home ground of Thames Iron Works Football Club, the team that became West Ham United in 1900. The event was marred by tragedy as the *East Ham Echo* of Friday 24 July 1903 reported under the headline 'Motor Track Fatality'.

At the West Ham Coroner's Court on Friday, Mr George E. Hilleary, the West Ham Coroner, held an inquest on the body of James Adams, aged 31, of 31 Larch Road, Cricklewood, who met his death at the Memorial Sports Ground, Canning Town, on Wednesday, July 15. Mr Percy J.H. Robinson watched the proceedings on behalf of the Ormonde Motor Company, one of whose machines the deceased was riding.

James Simms, the ground man at the Memorial Grounds, said that on Wednesday at about three o'clock the deceased and another man went on the ground with motorcycles. Witness knew they were coming, and asked, 'if they were going for the records?' Deceased said, 'No. We will wait till Mr Goodwin comes, but we are going to try the machines.' They rode round the track, each on separate motors, no one else being on the track. Deceased afterward went round twice; had he gone round a third time he would have done a mile. In witness's opinion the pace was from 50 to 60 miles an hour on the second lap. At the third lap it seemed as if the deceased was going at such a speed that his machine gave from under him, or that he lost control of it. He was no sooner off the motor than he was spinning round. His head struck a post. Witness saw blood and at once sent for a cart, and with assistance took deceased to West Ham Hospital.

A Juryman: Can they do as they like on the track? – There's the rule of all one-way, but they can go at what speed they like.

Arthur Goodwin, of 79, Wells Street, Oxford Street, manager of the Ormonde Motor Company, said the deceased was not on the track at or by his direction. As the jury knew, there had been races in Ireland, and at the meetings the Ormonde machines had been very successful. And when they came back they were thought to be good enough to secure World records. Mr Adams, an expert rider, asked if he could ride for the records, and it was agreed to let him try the machine … Deceased and the other man each rode about two miles; then they both dismounted and rested for a time, and went on again. Witness saw the accident – he was watching the rider most closely – and his impression was, he felt thoroughly convinced of it, that the speed developed so much that the rider could not realise the great rate. When he came to the bend, he took it perfectly clean, and from witness's observation the machine simply skidded clean from under him. He 'twizzled' round on his stomach 30 or 40 yards along and up the slope till he came to the fence. The machine was hardly damaged, the friction had flattened the handle-bar and fired it, and the saddle was grazed with friction, but the mechanism was all in order.

Before he started the second time witness asked the deceased what he thought to the machine, and he said, 'I think this is very fast; I think it is good enough for the World record; arrangements would have to be made for that. They were not supposed to know the speed limit of machines; it was impossible for anyone to know the limit of the speed of the machines, so much depended on the rider. The deceased was a perfectly good rider, sound and cool-headed.

A Juryman: The slope was not sufficient to keep the machine in its place? – Quite so.

Then it is the fault of the track? – The track was built for cycle riding, never for motor riding.

The Coroner: What speed do you say? – As near as I can tell from 60 to 65 miles an hour. It was a terrific pace.

Witness added that the deceased had ridden on the Crystal Palace track on a similar motor at 45 miles an hour, and he had made the remark that 'it was like touring, so easy to go round.' The Canning Town track was considered even better than the Crystal Palace track. On it had been won World records, and it was therefore assumed that it was the best track. He did not notice the 'wobbling' spoken of by one of the witnesses, who probably was misled by the usual 'lean over' of all cyclists in turning bends. Deceased had cleared the corner when the machine went away.

By Mr Robinson: The machine was the identical one that won the speed trial in Ireland, and the deceased knew that. Deceased was an amateur and got nothing from the company, who chose the Canning Town track because it held all the records for motors and cycles too.

The Coroner: What is the record?

Witness: It stands at 1min. 6sec. – roughly 58 miles an hour.
Mr Robinson: What was the horsepower of this machine?
Witness; It is impossible to say, it depends on the revolutions. Normally it was $3\frac{1}{4}$ hp. It was quite possible deceased was driving 2,000 revolutions, which would be equal to 4 hp .
The Coroner, in summing up said it was quite clear no track was a proper place for speed tests, or, indeed, for any excessive speeds. But expert riders were perfectly well aware of the risks they run. The jury then returned a verdict of 'Death from misadventure', and the foreman said it was the wish of the jury that no slur should be cast on the Canning Town track as a cycling track worthy of its reputation.

Anyone who knows speedway will recognise much of the glory, dangers, techniques and criticisms of oval racing in this report. It is a testament to the history that the sport has in London's East End and indicates that the essential elements of short-track motorcycle racing were in place from the time when motorcycles first sped across the face of the planet.

The Birth Of Speedway – The Workers' Racing

Speedway can be understood as a product of or a response to road racing, although even when controlled and administrated by a common governing body, a dichotomy is evident. Road racing was largely pioneered in Europe. The first generation of race drivers were, in the main, from the higher echelons of society. They were professionals and/or members of the gentry. The development of propulsion by way of the internal combustion engine in Europe took place on a relatively advanced system of roads, so it was logical to use the existing road networks for place-to-place races, and city-to-city races became extremely popular as the twentieth century began. This type of contest became firmly established in the mind of the general public as the preserve of gentlemen, the only group that had the time and the finance that the sport demanded.

In the early days, France was generally regarded as the home of the motorcar and, as such, Paris became the starting point for many of the long-distance contests. Paris to Berlin, Paris to Amsterdam and Paris to Vienna were among these early road marathons. They were not without dangers, and after the terrible events and near carnage of the Paris to Madrid race of 1903, open-road racing was effectively abandoned to be replaced by the closed-road circuit competitions. This started the sport on the evolutionary road that has given rise to the contemporary Grand Prix circuit and its association with massive development and staging costs.

Motorcycles have been a feature of organised oval-track events for over a hundred years all over the world. There are references (although confirmation as to their authenticity is not available) to forms of motorcycle short-track racing, on a circuit with a loose dirt surface, in Pietermaritzburg, Natal, South Africa in the spring of 1907, but, geographically speaking, the sport has three main strands of development.

14

The American Dream

Speedway, as a generic discipline, is a product of the USA. It was there, just after the First World War, that the sounds and smells of motorcycle oval racing became evident in any meaningful and consistent way (the expression 'speedway' was first used in the American context in 1902). As early as 1906, motorbikes were racing on the American fairground circuits under the auspices of the Federation of American Motorcyclists. By the early 1920s, these events had evolved into racing on huge dirt tracks (thus the term 'dirt-track racing' came into existence) originally laid down for racing horses. Many of the tracks were a mile or even more to the lap, but the majority were half-milers. It was the very size of these circuits that discouraged any attempts to surface them. The spectacle was a big public draw and highly dangerous, with riders using giant 1,000cc machines. Such high-powered apparatus needed superb riders, and the Americans certainly rose to the demand. These bulky hulks, with their 'vertical' handlebars, did not allow for any measure of broadsiding. The technique of cornering was to roll around the bend, with a little throttle and the wheels in line – similar to the road-racing style.

There was keen competition between manufacturers, such as the Harley-Davidson, Excelsior, Indian, Peerless and Cleveland companies. These, and other companies, retained professional riders to regularly race on improvised or loose surfaced tracks, which, despite precautions such as the spraying of light oil or calcium chloride on the surface, threw up voluminous clouds of dust. This, together with dangerous fences, inevitably caused fatalities, obliging organisers to limit competition machines to 500cc.

The introduction of smaller capacity motors permitted a more spectacular method of cornering. It was called the pendulum skid: a kind of power slide, which came to be known as broadsiding. This enabled a rider to negotiate a 180-degree turn on a powerful machine in a controlled skid in which the rear of the bike swung out – like a pendulum – and then back into line as the turn was completed.

The credit for the innovation of broadsiding has been given to a man by the name of Maldwyn Jones, an Excelsior and Harley-Davidson rider in 1922. During that year, other 500cc aces also became accomplished at the new technique. One of these was Eddie Brinck, who was killed while racing at Springfield in August 1927. After a couple of years, the smaller engine machines (500cc) were being raced everywhere in the United States, and broadsiding was recognised as the swiftest way of rounding the dirt track bends. It became the basic art of speedway racing.

Towards the end of 1925, 350cc racing machines made their debut on the Milwaukee dirt track, including the Harley-Davidson and Indian 350cc road models modified for racing purposes. These events caused a great sensation. In the Harley range, the 21 cubic-inch 'Peashooters', as they were named, averaged over 69mph in five-mile races; they were just two seconds slower than the famous 500cc bikes.

Advance Australia Fair

An early form of motorcycle track racing in Australia dates back to 1909, around a quarter-mile slightly banked asphalt track in Maitland, in the Hunter River Valley, before the track was closed in 1917. However, that same year grass-track racing was held at the nearby Newcastle Show Ground and during 1918, Sydney and interstate riders turned up to do battle with the locals on the one-mile racecourse at Wallsend, New South Wales.

For all this, while the development of dirt-track technology and style was going on in the USA, it was in rural New South Wales, back in the Hunter River Valley, under flood-lights at West Maitland Agricultural Showground on the 15 December 1923, that the first incarnation of modern short-track solo motorcycle racing (that was to become universally accepted as speedway), took place. The person behind the event was a New Zealander, one John S. Hoskins, better known as 'Johnnie'. This restless and energetic man was to become the accepted father of the sport. His life story accompanies the tale of West Ham Speedway and the sport's overall history. It was Hoskins who organised the West Maitland 'Electric Light Carnival' that took place that evening, celebrating the then recent installation of electricity in West Maitland. He decided to add interest to the event by including short-track motorcycle racing on a quarter-mile dirt surface. Few rules would encumber the adventurous spirit and ingenious spontaneity of speedway's first contestants, although riders were instructed that they could not put their foot down to help their stripped down road machines round corners. Australians always called their dirt-tracking 'speedway' – the British did not officially adopt the title until 1930.

The success of the meeting led Hoskins to conclude that he could make what started out as something of a gimmick into a new and exciting form of racing. More meetings were organised at West Maitland, and it came to be acknowledged as the birthplace of speedway. The sport reached out across New South Wales to Newcastle and, more impor-tantly, to Sydney. The organisation of events became more stylish and sophisticated. The Australian riders of the time, that included the now-legendary figures of Vic Huxley, Billy Lamont, and Frank Arthur, were reinforced by a some American pioneers – most notably the gigantic (in height as well as talent) Sprouts Elder.

Speedway's origins then can be understood as being set distinctly within a particular working culture and as such are very different from road racing. Speedway, like other forms of oval tracking, is essentially the product of the rural, new frontier countries colonized by Britain and other European powers. North America and Australia were as enthusiastic as Europe about automotive competition, but their circumstances were very different. They were countries built on a continental scale. Their road networks were, at best, sketchy. Those roads that did exist were often little more than rutted dirt tracks, unsuited to the type of racing that developed in Europe. Land, however, was not in short supply and not, as was the case in Britain, mainly in the hands of a landed aristocracy or gentry. Early enthusiasts in America and Australia found it a simple matter to mark out basic dirt courses on which anyone who wished could race. Motor races were very often associated with carnivals and local fairs, and most fairgrounds had show rings or dirt horseracing ovals. Car and bike racing on these tracks was a natural development and became tremendously popular.

As such, it can be seen that the geographical character of the frontier countries placed ordinary workers in the forefront of motor sport to a much greater extent than their

The 1924 programme for the first ever speedway meeting in Maitland, New South Wales, Australia.

BICYCLE & MOTOR CYCLE
CARNIVAL
Maitland Show Ground,
SATURDAY NIGHT, FEB. 9th, 1924

PROMOTED BY
H R.A. and H. ASSOCIATION.

UNDER PERMIT N.S.W. LEAGUE OF WHEELMEN.
Motor Cycle Events Controlled, Hamilton Motor Cycle Club.

EVENT NO. 1—
BRUSH HUNT (Over 3 ft. Hurdles) Prize £3. 2nd £1 from Prize.
Post entry 1/-.
Won by .... 2nd .... 3rd .... Time ....
HALF MILE BICYCLE HANDICAP (2 Laps). Prizes £6, £3 10/6
10/. 1st and 3 fastest 2nds start in Final.

European counterparts, but the nature of the social hierarchy also had an impact. The entrepreneur, not the landed gentry, topped the social strata. This social group was more focused on the development of business than the sporting pursuits associated with the European 'leisured classes'.

One result of all this is that speedway has often been associated with rowdy fairground activity and been projected as a slightly seedy, downmarket pastime. Historically, it has been considered to be rather less than respectable by sections of the motor racing establishment. However, this has meant that speedway never lost its working-class roots and, perhaps more than any other sport, has remained true to itself.

The British Experience

If America was the mind of speedway and Australia the soul, Britain has been where the body of the sport was established and where it found a home. There are reports of a form of speedway racing being held in England, at Portman Road football ground at Ipswich, in 1904, but it was only when reports of the new Australian daredevil sport filtered through to Britain that it started to become the seedbed of speedway in Europe. However, exactly how the sport arrived in the country remains a controversial question. The Speedway Control Board had it that a licence was granted by the Auto-Cycle Union (ACU) for a meeting at Camberley Heath in Surrey on 7 May 1927 (the local club claimed credit for many new events, including scrambles and even football on motorcycles). They staged an event subsequently described in *Motor Cycling* as: 'the first British Dirt-Track Meeting. However, the day's races were run the 'wrong way round' on a surface of loose sand and as such it would appear to have had more of a resemblance to modern grass-track racing than speedway. There was even a race with pillion passengers and Fay Taylour (a woman) was the winner of the unlimited final.

Northern followers claim the first British speedway meeting took place at Dodds Farm, Droylsden, near Manchester, on 25 June 1927. This meeting, organised by the enterprising South Manchester Motor Club, took place on a 550-yard cinder trotting track. Once again though, it is said that riders raced in a clockwise direction and that the event bore little resemblance to a modern speedway meeting.

High Beech, the birth-place of British speedway.

As such, speedway is understood to have put down its roots in the East London/West Essex area, when a race meeting was organised at the King's Oak track (an abandoned running/cycle track) at High Beech in Epping Forest, Essex on 19 February 1928. The track was situated behind the present day King's Oak public house and a conservation centre now stands on the site. Of all the 'dirt-track type' events that took place in the late 1920s, the King's Oak contest approximated most closely the look and feel of what was to become modern speedway. Jack Hill-Bailey, the secretary of the Ilford Motor Cycle Club, was the person behind this historic meeting, although the King's Oak track was by no means his first choice of venue. Custom House Stadium, the edifice that was to become the home of West Ham Speedway, that had opened in 1928, was initially chosen to stage the event. However, the stadium was built primarily for greyhound racing and the owners of the arena were loath to open their new venue with anything other than a greyhound meeting. This somewhat defensive attitude prevented the impressive stadium from providing an inspiring stage for the first ever speedway meeting in Britain.

Hill-Bailey, in talks with Lionel Wills and Keith MacKay, had also attempted to stage races at Parsloes Park, a half-mile trotting track near his home, in Barking, Essex, about two miles down the road from Custom House. He was not able to pull this off, but if this idea had been successful, High Beech would have never gained its distinction as the birthplace of the sport in Britain – although neither would Parsloes Park as the track would have been too long.

So, Hill-Bailey moved on to his third choice. Initially, he had planned an open permit event at High Beech for 9 November 1927, but the ACU would not grant permission for racing on a Sunday. A large number of entrants were disappointed, particularly so following all the false starts, to the extent that many would-be competitors were ready to go ahead and stage a meeting in defiance of the authority.

Eventually, Hill-Bailey, working with the Colchester Motor Cycle Club, obtained a permit from the ACU for the meeting, which was issued to the Ilford Motorcycle Club (this was the first meeting to be staged after the new ACU sub-committee responsible for licensing tracks had come into being). The application list was opened once more, and the response was immediate. First-rate riders from far and near applied to take part.

Hill-Bailey was expecting about 3,000 spectators to turn up, so 2,000 tickets and 500 programmes had been printed. When he arrived at 8 a.m., a crowd of 2,000 was already gathered in front of the King's Oak Hotel. Hill-Bailey was amazed, given that there were still two-and-a-half hours to go before the start.

The crowds kept coming. With an hour to go, all tickets had been sold, as had the last of the programmes. The cash booth had been swept aside and eager spectators were pouring in, some, equipped with pliers and metal cutters to be used to breach the barbed wire surrounding the ground. It became clear that the collection of further admission fees was unrealistic. With thirty minutes left before the event was due to start, 15,000 people were inside the track and thousands more were streaming along the lanes approaching the King's Oak track. Every police station within a radius of ten miles was alerted for reinforcements as the crowds jammed the roads out of East London.

Hill-Bailey had considered that the event would be of little interest outside East London and Essex, but his expectations with regard to the number of potential spectators turned out to be a woeful underestimate as more than 30,000 people turned up to watch the day's proceedings. It is surprising that the attendance was so poorly forecast. Just five years before, West Ham United, a football club with its root support in the East London/West Essex area, had attracted close to 250,000 spectators to Wembley for their first FA Cup final appearance against Bolton Wanderers.

The ACU had insisted that all spectators should be confined behind a rope barrier on the inside of the track, but such was the crush that the rule was unenforceable, with spectators swarming round the inside and outside of the circuit.

The initial races were described as hell on wheels. Many competitors were trials riders and considered it unethical to allow their feet to touch the ground. Johnnie Hoskins had been in England with a group of Australian riders for a short while and two were present at High Beech that day, Billy Galloway and Keith MacKay. They demonstrated the art of leg-trailing or broadsiding, by then the accepted form of cornering in Australia. Their appearance had not been advertised by Hill-Bailey – had he done so, the crowd may well have reached 60,000. One of the British riders at this historic meeting was Phil Bishop. Many years later he would ride for and manage West Ham Speedway.

The *Daily Mirror*, who became one of the most consistent sponsors of speedway, covered the very first meeting held in Britain the next morning. Pictures of the action and the crowd were accompanied by a report that included the following: 'Dirt-track motor-cycle racing, the sport popular in Australia, where it rivals greyhound racing, was seen in England for the first time yesterday at King's Oak Speedway, High Beech near Loughton. The size of the crowd was a surprise.'

The event pushed Bluebird and Sir Malcolm Campbell's (at the time, Captain Campbell) new World land speed record of 206.596mph into second place on the front page.

Daily Mirror

GREAT NEW SERIAL BEGINS TO-DAY ON PAGE 15

£10,000

ENGLAND'S FIRST SIGHT OF AUSTRALIA'S BIG SPORT

In the beginning there was Johnny.. he's still going strong

Where it all started . . . High Beech on February 19, 1928. And the curious fans flocked in.

ASK any inhabitants of the little Essex hamlet of High Beech, on the fringe of Epping Forest, what happened on Sunday, February 19, 1928, and they will tell you that was the day speedway racing was born.

To be precise, it was the day when some forty or more motorcycle clubmen met for two-wheel combat, watched by an estimated 30,000 crowd behind the King's Oak Hotel.

But was this really the birth of a sport that is marking its fiftieth anniversary with a Golden Jubilee meeting at Hackney on Sunday?

Friends in the North of England will hotly dispute the claim. They say that the first dirt-track meeting was staged by the South Manchester motor-cycle club on June 25, 1927, at Droylsden trotting track, which was a third of a mile long and had banked bends.

Growth

A year later, they will also claim, 42,000 spectators watched dirt-tracking in Manchester—on the day that Britain's first stadium built for Speedway was opened. They were not all at the new track around Belle Vue greyhound course. In fact only 15,000 were there; the other 27,000 were at the White City track.

But the crowd in the White City was an indication of the astonishing growth of the sport in little more than a year after its inception at High Beech—or Droylsden.

Whatever opinion you may hold about the origin of official Speedway racing in Britain—and I tend to favour the claim of High Beech—there isn't much doubt about who brought the sport to this country.

By DON CLARKE

A rumbustious Australian named John S. Hoskins, now in his 86th year and still going strong as a promoter of today's National League club Canterbury, claims the honour. And no one will deny it.

There will never be another Johnny Hoskins. Since 1923 he has been building and operating tracks in Australia, England, Scotland, Spain and America. A great spectacle on race nights is Hoskins, dishevelled and spotted with cinder dust, leaning over the pit gates bellowing instructions at his men—who, of course, can't hear a word he is saying.

The flow of adjectives, not always complimentary, that greet the unsuccessful have to be heard to be believed. Yet Johnny is a lovable character, and there is nothing his men will not do for him. In fact riders think he is sickening for something if he doesn't create.

Hoskins was often the butt of riders' pranks. His hat bill must have been astronomical, because riders would not hesitate to soak his large Stetson with petrol and set it alight, then proceed to douse both the flames and Hoskins with buckets of water.

Temper

Stories of Johnny's deeds and misdeeds are numerous, but a typical example concerns a Test match at Sydney. The match was being fought under rolling start conditions in which all riders were supposed to get away level. When Australians Billy Lamont and Arnie Hansen came out in opposition to Jack Parker and Wally Philips there wasn't much in it.

The Aussies were determined not to let the Englishmen poach a lead, and there was one false start after another. Eventually Johnny lost his temper. He stopped the race and rushed on the track to lay down the law.

"I'm going to start this race by standing in the middle in front of the starting line. You will pass slowly two on one side and two on the other. Don't accelerate until you have passed me," he ordered.

The riders nodded their agreement, but their thoughts must have been miles away because they came up at full throttle. Hoskins stood there petrified. The riders were on top of him before he could move.

Three swerved round on the track to miss him. Billy Lamont dived for the inside only to catch Johnny in the seat of

Johnny Hoskins...brimful of confidence in his heyday, and (right) the happy veteran.

his pants with his handlebars. Johnny was tossed as high as the track lights. Billy finished up in the safety fence!

Among the band of Australians who brought the sport to England in 1928 were Vic Huxley, Frank Arthur, Charlie Spinks, Frank Pearce, Jack Bishop, Hilary Buchanan, Dickie Smythe, Ben Unwin (all Queenslanders) and Billy Lamont (New South Wales).

They held a supremacy which was not seriously challenged until 1930 when Jack Parker, Eric Langton, Frank Varey, Jim Kempster, Colin Watson, Roger Frogley, Squib Burton and Syd Jackson began to show their former masters a clean pair of wheels.

But from a big money point of view most English riders, with the possible exception of Jack Parker and Eric Langton, missed the gravy train. During 1928 and 1929 staggering sums were paid to Australian and American riders, the racing aristocracy, to appear at a track. The keenest businessman of them all was America's Lloyd "Sprouts"

Elder. When he agreed to ride for Southampton in the League he demanded, and got, £1,000, and in his three years of racing he tucked away the best part of £50,000.

The other star in the £50,000 class was Vic Huxley, who had a tremendous run of success. For six consecutive years he was in the top half-dozen, and consistently averaged £200 to £300 a week.

Dubious

Most of these old-timers used their winnings sensibly, but with some it was a case of easy come, easy go. Hundreds of pounds earned in a few minutes were gambled away in even less time. Some riders acquired a stable of high-powered cars with the sole object of belting across the country faster than the next man.

Others showered their girl friend of the moment with expensive gifts, or unwisely invested in risky stock market ventures and dubious night clubs. Fortunately, that phase soon passed, and order gradually emerged from chaos.

Rider on the left at High Beech is Vic Huxley. Billy Lamont stands between the bikes.

TOMORROW: THE LEG-TRAILERS

It all started at the King's Oak Hotel.

The results of the event were:

Event 1: Novice (5 laps)
1st   Fred Ralph (344 Coventry-Eagle), 2m 20s
2nd   Ivor Creek(490 Norton)
3rd   H.M. Smyth (493 Sunbeam)

Event 2: Solo (5 laps)
1st   Alf Foulds (493 Sunbeam), 2m 2s
2nd   Billy Galloway (494 Douglas)

Event 3: Sidecars (5 laps):
C.M. Harley (488 Zenith sc.), 2m 29s

Event 4: Novices (3 laps)
1st   Ivor Creek (490 Norton), 1m 25s
2nd   Alan Day (493 Sunbeam)
3rd   G.Fletcher (557 Ariel)

Event 5: Solo (3 laps)
1st   Reg Pointer (497 Ariel), 1m 17s
2nd   A. Duce (343 Sunbeam)
3rd   P.R. Bradbrook (344 Coventry-Eagle)

Event 6: Sidecars (3 laps)
1st   Arthur Noterman (498 Triumph sc.), 1m 23.2s
2nd   Alf Foulds (493 Sunbeam sc.)
3rd   H. Lock (498 AJS sc.)

Event 7: cancelled owing to lack of time.

Event 8: Fastest Lap from Standing Start
(Solo)
1st   W. Medcalf (348 Douglas), 26.8s
2nd   A. Foulds (493 Sunbeam), 27s
3rd   F.R. Pointer (497 Ariel), 27.2s
(Sidecars)
1st   A. Noterman (498 Sunbeam sc.), 30s
2nd   L.J. Pellat (344 O.K.-Supreme sc.), 30.6s
3rd   A. Foulds (493 Sunbeam Sc.), 31.65

As can be seen, Reg Pointer had a good day in the solo event. He was amongst the most prominent English riders of the early period. He went on to ride for International Speedways and was a popular figure at Wimbledon and White City, where he had good successes in handicap events. He started out riding an Ariel but took up the Rudge Special later in his career.

Also at the High Beech that day was Jack Parker, on behalf of manufacturers BSA. Both he and his brother Norman were 'works' supported trials riders: Jack for BSA and Norman for New Hudson. Jack won the Colmore Cup in 1928 on a BSA and also represented Great Britain in the International Six-Day Trial. Within weeks of King's Oak, both Jack and Norman commenced speedway careers that would last over twenty years and would see them form one of the most formidable partnerships ever fielded in an England team. During the 1929 and 1930 seasons, both Jack and Norman rode for Coventry. The track was on the Brandon site, the original site being under the back straight of the modern stands.

Norman Parker was born on 14 January 1908 in Birmingham. In the 1920s, this was not only 'the workshop of the Empire', it was also a centre for motorcycle manufacture and Norman grew up to become part of this, as an international-class trials rider, a professional speedway rider and team manager, a garage owner, a haulage contractor and a publican. He was one of the best English riders until the late 1940s. He was still competing at Swindon in the mid-1950s.

The High Beech track continued for some years after its first event. The 1929 High Beech Champion was Jack Barnett. Not long afterwards he won the Golden Gauntlet at West Ham, beating Sprouts Elder and Roger Frogley in the final, despite being last on the first lap. Frogley dropped out during the third run round and, before the end of the race, Elder had broken

down. The local boy came home as champion and as he did his lap of honour wearing the Gauntlet the fans spilt onto the track in their hundreds to congratulate him. The early days of dirt-track riding were dominated by a number of riders that started at High Beech, including Ron Howes, Howdy Byford, Vic Gooden and Brian Meredith, as well as pioneers such as Syd Edmonds and Buddy Lexton. It was to become something of an unofficial 'feeder club' for the West Ham Speedway team.

Phil Bishop, following a winning run.

Jack Parker, captain of Belle Vue.

Ironically, the next important speedway event was the first ever meeting hosted at Custom House Stadium in July 1928 (some sources claim that this took place in 1929, but newspapers of the time, including the *Leytonstone Express*, show 1928 to be the correct date). Possibly the profit potential exemplified at High Beech outweighed the somewhat sectarian mentality that had held up history earlier in the year. Greyhound racing was first held at the stadium on 4 August 1928.

The Legacy

Although Australia was the birthplace of the sport, after the huge success of speedway meetings in England in the 1930s and 1940s, Britain was to become the home of the short, oval, loose-surfaced track motorbike racing. Following the revival of speedway in the late 1960s, strenuous efforts were made to spread the speedway gospel to far-flung parts of the world. Although it has had a chequered history since its birth, the meteoric growth of speedway was phenomenal. In 1971, speedway's World Championship attracted entries from nineteen countries and tracks were appearing in Africa and North and South America – but at times the sport has been in danger of extinction in its major centre, Britain. The crises seemed to be over by the start of the 1970s, sadly not before the demise of West Ham's contribution. This is when the sport emerged as one of Britain's top spectator attractions, drawing an estimated 150,000 spectators each week. This firm base, combined with expanding international horizons, seemed to assure speedway a rosy future as the twentieth century entered its final quarter.

The appeal of speedway is that it really is about racing. When spectators paid their money at the turnstiles they got to see all the action, not just a fleeting glimpse of competitors as they flashed past a particular vantage point. The concept and experience might be basic, but its immediacy and raw excitement was hard to match. That is what made it such an attraction and why, over the years, millions have flocked to their local tracks week after week.

Maybe your heart was at its happiest on the bleachers at Eldorain, Ohio, or your spirit may have soared around the grassy banks of Wagga Wagga Raceway. You may still feel the thrill of being in the stands of Brisbane Exhibition Showgrounds, or perhaps had

Hammer Howdy Byford.

some of your best times watching West Ham Speedway from the terracing of Custom House Stadium. Although the sport has, in many ways, been very fragmented, speedway people, the whole world over, have much in common. They are united in their love of the race, the romance of speed and the thrill and power that the combination of human and machine can bring into being.

Speedway has trodden a difficult, if exciting, path over its seventy years or so years and, like most minority sports, has always had to fight for survival. It has enjoyed the advantage of being reasonably well organised under the auspices of a single international sanctioning body, but it seems likely that in the future the sport will have to survive the same trials and tribulations that have plagued it since its first days in the frontier environments of Australia and America.

1

THE FIRST SPEEDWAY DAYS

The Starting Marshall

This is the man who stands behind the starting tapes and beckons the riders up to the line with outstretched arms. His job is not as simple as it looks. He must see that all the riders are in their correct starting positions and that all are ready to race, before signalling them to approach the tapes. He must then ensure that all riders come to a dead stop in the proper place. When he is completely satisfied that all is correct, he will then drop his arms and walk away from the starting gate, thus signalling to the referee that all the riders are ready and in a proper position to start. The referee will then switch on the green light and start the race by raising the tapes. However, the Starting Marshall is not finished yet. He is also responsible for counting the laps and showing the appropriate flags – yellow for 'One more lap to go' and checked for the finish – in addition to any other warning flags that the referee may instruct him to use such as the black disqualification flag, or, much more common, the red flag to stop a race. So you can see that he has to be on his toes throughout the meeting with never a dull moment!

Silver, L. 'The Starting Marshall' in *The Speedway Annual* compiled by Silver, L. and Douglas, P. (London, Pelham Books, 1969)

After speedway was launched in Britain with the fabulous, almost impromptu, event at High Beech in February 1928, West Ham Speedway, at Custom House Stadium, was one of the first places to present the sport in an organised way. Having moved his operation from Celtic Park in Glasgow, Jimmy Baxter, the driving force behind Dirt-Track Speedways Ltd, promoted the first meeting at Custom House on 28 July 1928. Alderman Jack Jones MP officially opened the track. The press were optimistic and supportive, reporting that:

A colossal crowd saw this opening of the West Ham Stadium for dirt track racing on Saturday afternoon. Dirt Track Speedways Ltd. are running the venture and they provided an excellent afternoon's sport, though at times the organisation failed to stand the strain. This is almost always the case at the opening meetings, however.

Paddy Dean won the West Ham Invitation Handicap that day. Dean, an Australian champion, first started riding in the mid-1920s. He performed at most of the better-known tracks in Australia and, in September 1927, broke the track record at the Speedway Royal, Sydney. He then came over to ride for Dirt-Track Speedways Ltd. He was to become one of the most popular riders at the West Ham track, winning many of the big handicaps and trophy races. He made the headlines when he broke the record for the Crystal Palace track. Dean had beaten the lean, flamboyant, larger-than-life Sprouts Elder into second place in the Handicap, after the great American champion – possibly the biggest draw of his day – had lost a lot of time at the start. However, Elder made up for his misfortune by taking the main event of the day, the track championship, winning the Golden Gauntlet. Elder, who could command £100 to take part in an event (a tremendous sum in those days), was one of the tallest riders during the first years of speedway. He started racing in the USA and rapidly attained prominence on the big American tracks, securing many trophies and records. He came to England in 1928, with Johnnie Hoskins and his Australian riders. Sprouts wasn't just a star rider but a spectacular leg-trailer and he became one of the best known speedway names competing in England. He rode as a freelance before league competition was established, but later turned out for West Ham, White City and Stamford Bridge. Sprouts Elder eventually joined the board of management at West Ham, but he still maintained his freelance approach to racing.

Also taking part in the events at Custom House that day in July 1928 was Mart Sieffert; he was a very cool-headed rider and was a familiar figure on most English tracks in the later 1920s. He was one of the riders who turned out at the first British speedway meeting at King's Oak. Sieffert competed in the Silver Sash and the Silver Wheel and was to be a winner of the West Ham All-Comers Handicap.

Probably England's finest dirt-track rider of the early period, Ivor Creek, was another contributor to the first speedway event at Custom House. After competing at King's Oak in 1928, he went from strength to strength. In a memorable Match Race with Billy Galloway, he appeared to have the race all wrapped up from the second lap, but there was very little daylight between them at the finish.

The Indian

According to *The Motor Cycle* of 2 August 1928, Art Pecher had trouble with his Indian bike at West Ham's inaugural dirt-track event (but, in any case, he was not at his best on a bumpy track like West Ham). Indian motorcycles were initially raced as early as 1915, on steeply banked wooden-board tracks and the huge one-mile fairground dirt tracks in the USA. Cecil Brown, an American, was an adherent of the Indian, doing much to popularise the bike. He was among the first international stars to appear in Australia when dirt-track racing took hold there in the mid-1920s. Born in Manistique, Michigan, Brown started racing at seventeen and for three years was undefeated on the big American tracks. He went to Australia in 1925 and, on his Indian, Brown rode with phenomenal success at such racetracks as Penrith (a one-mile track near Sydney) and a half-mile circuit at Newcastle, where he secured the three-mile Australian Dirt-Track Championship. On the unique 1,540-yard, extremely banked (and lethal) concrete saucer in the Sydney beach-side suburb of Manoubra, he had great success, winning the

Golden Helmet seven times and taking the two-mile Australian Championship at Cessnock. Few other riders had more experience than Brown of different kinds of track riding.

When speedway first arrived in England in 1928, another Indian rider to become an early star was Art Pechar, who tore around the smaller British tracks. In its traditional red trim, the features on this machine included a lever throttle (no twist grip), a padded hook for the right leg, absolute minimal suspension and an exhaust pipe measuring no more than five inches – some like it hot! Pechar was known as the American Crack. He was born in Tarry Town, New York in 1901 and started racing at the age of eighteen. In 1926, he entered 27 races and won 23 of them. A year later, just before leaving for Britain, he held the American three- and ten-mile National Dirt-Track Championships on a half-mile track. The first time he appeared in England, he broke both the Greenford and Stamford Bridge track records in the one day. During his short stay in England, he rode with great success on most tracks and was well supported at Stamford Bridge.

Roger Frogley was another Custom House debutant. He was to make a name for himself on the Crystal Palace Speedways and was one of the finest English riders of the pre-1930 era. He first came into prominence early in 1928, when riding at Stamford Bridge – where some marvellous performances enabled him to win many prestigious handicap and trophy races. He also had a good deal of success on the West Ham track,

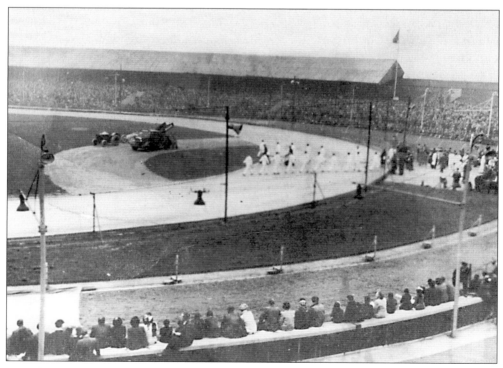

Marching out at West Ham from the pits on the first bend.

Phil Bishop in his 'leg-trailer' incarnation.

notably defeating Australian Charlie Spinks in a Match Race. This was no mean feat. Spinks had a spectacular (and some said reckless) way of broadsiding, which made him extremely popular at most big-track meetings before 1930. He had also, in the same month as West Ham's first meeting, broken the lap record at the Harringay track (19.7 seconds) and won the Silver Wheel and Silver Wings trophies.

However, one of the biggest attractions for the supporters on that summer's day seventy-five years ago was the first star of the speedways and the darling of the crowds from the day he started in the sport at West Maitland (his home state) in 1924. Billy Lamont first saw light in Newcastle, New South Wales. Arguably the greatest of all the dirt-track riders of the early period, 'Cyclone Billy', a winner of the *News of the World* belt at Crystal Palace, was famous for his 'neck or nothing' style that made him the sensation of the first English season and of practically every country where speedway had gained a foothold. During his career, he broke almost all Australian records and won many of the most prestigious titles. He came to England with International Speedways and took several track records, including an impressive performance at Stamford Bridge. When in action he was one of the most exciting of riders to watch, invariably smashing into the bends at full throttle. Although his worldwide activities interrupted Billy Lamont's English career, he rode for Wimbledon and Clapton League teams before joining Wembley in 1935, transferring to Nottingham in 1937. His best international match performance was in the Second Test of 1932, riding for Australia, when his partnership with Dicky Case was unbeaten.

Operating in its first season on an open licence basis, West Ham thus took its place in the speedway circuit alongside Wimbledon, White City, Stamford Bridge, Crystal

Palace, and, a little later, Wembley in the South and Manchester's Belle Vue track in the North. The stadium soon got into its four-events-a-week routine of a speedway meeting, a card of stock-car racing and two greyhound meetings.

Mechanical Evolution

The speedway machine that was used in the mid-1930s did not look very different from those that were ridden forty years on at the end of West Ham's speedway days. They were different, of course, but the changes that were made were subtle, taking place over many years, and were usually adaptations of the original model to changing tracks and accommodating modern technology. The men that built them didn't change much either. In the late 1960s, there was at least one expert 'tuner' at West Ham who had been practising his trade since 1928.

In the late 1920s and early 1930s, the most exciting years in the history of the sport, there was no such thing as a marketed speedway motorcycle in Britain. Riders followed the Australian pattern of stripping down and modifying their ordinary road machines for speedway meetings. But it soon became plain that specialised machinery was necessary for such a specific type of racing. Initially, Norton, BSA and Velocette started offering 'speedway models'. Although some weight reduction was achieved by precluding fittings such as chain-cases and mudguards, these machines were road bikes with some modifications. For example, they had no brakes. In fact, a bike with brakes violated the rules of the sport. It was imperative to take away the temptation to 'put the anchors on' and so prevent the kind of incident that would take place if four riders were charging into a bend at break-neck speed and suddenly the leading man decelerated too rapidly.

By the end of 1928, seventeen well-known manufacturers were displaying speedway machinery at the London Motorcycle Show. At first, the Harley 'Peashooter' proved the most popular bike, but already several leading Australian riders had adopted modified Douglas machines. Douglas were the first concern to set about making a pure speedway motorcycle and, despite the efforts of well-known names such as AJS, BSA Cotton, New Imperial, Scott, and Triumph, their creation was selected by most of the star speedway riders. This horizontal twin-cylinder machine is still held in great affection by those who rode it or saw it raced, although it lasted only a short time as a top machine. It was supplanted by the Rudge, but this bike too, was destined for a short career.

As the speedway bike evolved, the gearbox was maintained, but intermediate gear pinions were removed, resulting in the option of only one gear. The countershaft, as it was known, carried a sprocket, which, like the engine sprocket and rear wheel sprocket was made so that it could be changed either between races or between meetings. Most riders did not change the countershaft sprocket in order to get a different gear ratio; they usually changed either the rear wheel sprocket or the engine sprocket. They changed gears because the larger tracks needed higher gears to allow the bike to move faster. Smaller tracks required lower gears so that the bike could accelerate more quickly. The gear ratio was sometimes changed between races in order to suit the track surface better. In broad principle, it can be said that the deep or heavy surface needed a lower gearing than the 'slick' or fine surface. Since the track surface might have changed according to weather conditions, a rider, even on his home track, did not always know what to expect and could sometimes arrive at a meeting with the incorrect gear ratio fitted to his machine.

The readers identified the gear ratio by a number, and this number was calculated by finding out the number of times the engine revolved to give one revolution of the rear wheel. Thus a 'low' gear might be 9.1 and a high gear might be 8.00. This means that the engine revolved 9.1 times to turn the rear wheel once in the case of the 'low' gear, but only 8 times in the case of the 'high' gear. The lower the number of times the engine revolved to get one turn of the rear wheel, the higher the gearing. To save time in calculations, each rider had a chart showing him which sprockets he needed to get the gearing he desired. At West Ham, a fairly big track, a rider would have fitted about 8.1 or 8.2, whilst at Oxford, a much smaller oval, he would have fitted about 8.8.

The application of larger diameter wheel rims also became a significant feature of the speedway bike. A larger wheel gave a greater 'arc of contact' – a longer strip of tyre tread in contact with the ground. This provided more efficient drive on the loose surface of the speedway track, which was important as in those early days the cinders could be as much as 4in in depth. The wheel sizes, 23in-diameter for the front wheel and 22in at the rear, become standard for the first quarter of a century of speedway bikes. One of the leading tyre manufacturers began to provide speciality tyres: for the front, these had a narrower section (2.75in) and were widely spaced, with taller longitudinal tread blocks. This gave a quite 'spiky' effect that helped the wheel maintain the direction in which its rider steered it. A unique tread (of wider section of 3.25in) was developed for the rear tyre. This had 'bands' of deep tread across the tyre and narrow longitudinal cuts. However, these bands of tread were not at right angles to the plane of the tyre, but ran across at an oblique angle. This caused the tread strips in contact with the track to be square to the direction of the front wheel (direction of travel), improving the driving force on the bends when the machine was cornering in broadside. Many grass-track riders also used these tyres, but in the days when right-hand bends were also to be found on grass tracks, the angled tread strips were in the wrong direction for cornering to the right, and the most expert broadsiders were restricted to relatively low speeds on right-hand bends.

The size of the speedway bike's fuel tank became much smaller than on other machines, as racing for just four laps only requires about half a gallon of fuel. An undersized tank holding less fuel makes the speedway bike comparatively light. The speedway bikes also used methanol – or, as the riders called it, 'dope' – for fuel, avoiding the carbon content of petrol, which provided a cleaner atmosphere for spectators. Methanol is composed of alcohol and other chemicals. It is faster burning than petrol and therefore cleaner, but it is only suitable for engines with a very high compression ratio, like that of a speedway bike. The bikes also used vegetable rather than mineral oils. All the oil that went into a speedway engine was fed out of the crankcases on to the track in a 'total loss' system; on a road machine, the oil is circulated round the engine and back to the oil tank for re-use. As such, the speedway engine had clean oil running through it all the time.

The emphasis on reducing weight has been a continual consideration in the design history of the track machine. From the earliest days, there was a quest to make the bike more compact: as such, the frame tubing became smaller as new and stronger alloys became available.

The First Expansion

After the spring of 1928, speedway blossomed all over the country and, by 1929, the sport was developing into an organised business. The great names of Australian speedway came to compete in Britain. Perhaps the most famous and influential of these first migrants was 'Wizard' Frank Arthur and Vic Huxley.

Frank Arthur was born in Lismore, New South Wales. He started racing at an early age, but he had to wait until 1927 for success. It was in this year that he surprised everyone by winning the Golden Helmet in Australia, when competing against some of the best-known riders. Arthur came to England to ride for International Speedways Ltd and carried off many top trophies – including the Golden Helmet, which at one point he had won more than any other man.

Starting his dirt-track racing career in 1926, Vic Huxley was one of the pioneers of speedway. He learnt to broadside in Brisbane, where he was born on 23 September 1906, and became one of the greatest exponents of the art. He really began to impress when riding the Harley Peashooter, becoming an overnight sensation at the 'Ekka', as well as the Toowoomba Showground and Davies Park in Brisbane. Huxley came to England to ride for International Speedways in 1928 and turned out for Wimbledon, White City and Hall Green (Birmingham), gaining the lap record for both Wimbledon and White City. He joined Harringay in 1930. He became almost unbeatable in the first few years of speedway, breaking records all over the country, including the one-mile standing start for Davies Park and the world's flying start record for the third-of-a-mile track. Huxley won eight £100 championships and the Golden Helmet on a number of occasions. He successfully defended his championship title against Colin Watson, but lost it to Jack Parker.

Peashooter Power

The Peashooter was also present when the sport was introduced to England in 1928. Riders to use the Harley included Frank Arthur and Buzz Hibberd. However, after the initial season, the British twin-cylinder Douglas outclassed the American bike.

Colin Watson, who had been a fine amateur footballer, was born in Ilford, Essex, of Scottish parents and was to become one of the most experienced riders in the pre-war period. Although he had been wounded in the First World War, he made impressive strides after taking part in the historic King's Oak event in 1928 and held several records for that track. Competing under the banner of International Speedways Ltd from 1929,

Watson first rode for White City and Harringay, and later joined the successful Wembley League side, skippering the team from 1930. He was also popular at Wimbledon, where he competed successfully in handicap events. Watson was not a spectacular stylist, but he was one of the safest and fastest of the homegrown riders of the pre-1930 period. In 1929, he began to ride the $2\frac{3}{4}$ Peashooter Harley, having bought his machine from Frank Arthur. Watson swept the board at the start of the 1931 season, but concussion in the last Test match of 1933 and a badly fractured leg at the start of the 1935 season held him back and prevented him from reaching his true potential in the years to come.

The Peashooter was a phenomenal machine. On the 556-yard Sydney Showground, Tommy Benstead won many prestige events on his Peashooter, even though he raced rivals on heavier 500cc machines. It remains one of the truly famous, all-time favourite dirt-track motorcycles. It is widely regarded as the first true thoroughbred racing speedway machine, rather than a modified road bike. It was originally coloured army green, with 'U'-shaped handlebars that faced the ground, as if to hunch the rider forward while power-sliding on dirt tracks. The bike excelled during the period when organised dirt-track racing began in the mid-1920s. In 1926, Harley Davidson factory rider Joe Petrali raced the Peashooter in the USA. It was a 350cc machine which, at 290lb, was a light bike, which meant superior handling. Soon the Peashooter was exported to Australia. Aussie pioneers Charlie Spinks and Frank Pearce, the first big stars at the Brisbane Exhibition Ground, made good use of the bike during its first season, 1926/27.

League Racing

Up to 1929, Custom House had fallen in line with all the other tracks of the period, the management serving up a diet of individual events, handicaps, scratch races and one- and two-lap time trials. The regular performers had included Ivor Creek, Jack Adams, Dell Forster, Billy Bragg and Buzz Hibberd, who, at around 6ft, was one of the tallest riders of his period. Hibberd came over to England from Australia in 1928 as a mechanic. He was born in Sydney and was an electrician by trade. However, when he got his chance, Hibberd showed himself to be a rider of great ability, winning the Golden Gauntlet in Glasgow and gaining good successes in

Tiger Stevenson.

Tommy Croombs zooms round the bend.

handicap racing. He further illustrated his pedigree by defeating Frank Pearce and Dicky Smythe in Match Races.

Frank C. Pearce was a fine Australian rider, who in November 1928 took the world record for a $2\frac{3}{4}$ machine, and was three times the winner of the Golden Helmet. Pearce probably had more experience of the racing track than any other rider before 1930. After coming to England with International Speedways Ltd., he met with a run of bad luck. Many times he was on the verge of a brilliant win, only to drop out as the result of mechanical problems with his bike, often involving broken chains.

'Flying Dicky Smythe' (his nickname was bestowed on him in recognition of his spectacular broadsiding technique) was a distant relative of Vic Smythe, the Epsom trainer – Dick had been a jockey before taking to the speedway tracks. He was one of the original band of Australians who brought speedway to England in 1928. He became a great favourite at White City and Wimbledon, winning the Golden and Silver Helmets. He broke the lap record for the Birmingham track and held the four-lap record for the Harringay and Manchester speedways. He returned to England in 1931 and 1932, to be hailed as one of the most exciting members of the Stamford Bridge team that became runners-up and then winners of the League. Particularly successful in 1932, he rode in all five Test matches of that year, before returning to his native Brisbane. However, Smythe came back to Wembley after three years of 'retirement'. Taking time to recover from a spinal injury sustained in a crash, he recovered his form riding for Harringay in 1936.

With the crowds drifting away, having become disenchanted with individual competition, it was Jimmy Baxter who set up team racing at Custom House Stadium. The

Hammers' first opponents were Southampton. The new format was a huge success. Baxter had persuaded his peers to organise a league and the West Ham Speedway team roared into existence in 1929, which was when legitimate inter-track competition and league racing competition started in Britain with the English Southern League. There were eleven founder members of the League, including eight London tracks.

League and team racing was thus a West Ham initiative that effectively saved speedway from an early demise, moving it away from its circus/fairground roots and giving it credibility as a sport. As a result, supporters began to develop a much closer relationship with competitors than was usual in other forms of motor sport. Fans identified with their teams in the same way as football supporters. The Speedway Hammers of West Ham commanded the same type of loyalty as their counterparts just down the road at Upton Park. Team racing enabled many young riders to cut their teeth on the track and soon British men like Roger Frogley and Colin Watson started to match the Australians.

The first Custom House and London League match took place on 2 May 1929. Coventry were the visitors. In the West Ham side that day were Taffy Williams, Jack Adams, Les Maguire, Reg Bounds, Don Taylor, Buzz Hibberd and captain Harold 'Tiger' Stevenson. Stevenson earned his nickname from his determination to succeed despite countless mishaps in his early days. He was introduced to the finer techniques of speedway by Sprouts Elder, whose sweeping spectacular style he emulated and refined, even when more efficient and austere styles became more widely deployed. 'Tiger' was to lead the West Ham side on many occasions.

The Hammers won their first match by a convincing 31-11 margin. Unfortunately, the team was unable to maintain this kind of form and finished their first season in sixth place, trailing well behind Stamford Bridge, who won 17 of their 20 contests. Soon, a Northern League was started and team racing became the main form of speedway competition.

It was during this first proper season that Buzz Hibberd encouraged a young mechanic who had just arrived in Britain from New South Wales to have a go at riding. At first the new youngster was not very impressive. He often fell and found the short-track sport hard to handle. However, by degrees the newcomer grew in confidence and technical ability and eventually broke into the side; Bluey Wilkinson had arrived.

Arthur Wilkinson ('Bluey' is an ironic Australian term of reference for a person with red hair) started life as a newsboy, but by 1930 he was one of the best riders in the country – commanding £100 a week as a speedway champion. Bluey spent his entire career with West Ham. He had an unorthodox style and indomitable spirit, frequently winning by sheer persistence and will. Sadly, the mentor was never to see the success of his protégé. Hibberd returned to Australia for the winter after the 1929 season and died in competition when his machine seized solid. A fraction of a second later, he was struck from behind by another rider and killed instantly.

West Ham nominated Sprouts Elder (Overseas) and Ivor Creek (England) for the Star Riders' Championship. This was the pre-1936 equivalent of the World Championship, sponsored by the *London Star* newspaper with the objective of determining the best individual rider of the day. From 1930 onwards, the contestants were drawn from the top twelve scorers from the first 15 league matches of the season. Three riders at a time lined up in eliminating races, culminating in a run-off between two riders.

Sprouts Elder won his first round match, beating Southampton's Billy Galloway, but in the semi-final, Vic Huxley was too good for him. Ivor Creek lost to the eventual winner, Roger Frogley, in the second round, having won his first round match with Tommy Croombs, then a rider at Lea Bridge. Croombs was a small, light and reserved man who left his job as a plasterer in New Malden to become a pioneer among British speedway riders with Brighton. He was one of the few early English riders to ride a Peashooter Harley successfully. After moving from Brighton, he broke the record for the Lea Bridge track in 1928, beginning his rapid rise to fame. He quickly became a scratch starter in many handicap races. His method of almost standing on his right footrest when going round the bends was reminiscent of Frank Arthur. Like Arthur, he kept very close to the white line, becoming known as the White Line Wizard because of his ability to hold the inside of the track at top speed. The quiet Croombs thrilled the Lea Bridge crowd for two years before joining the Hammers in 1930.

2

RUNNING ROUND IN CIRCLES

The Pushons
There can be any number of these men, the number usually varying according to the wishes of the promoter, or the quality of the men available. Like the rakers, they must be strong and preferably fairly tall, for their main task is to push the rider and his machine in order to get the engine started. This apparently simple task needs much more skill than one would at first think. Most young men who start this job without any previous experience find that they usually stop pushing much too soon. The common mistake is to stop pushing when he hears the engine start to splutter into life. The experienced pusher will know that it is at this time when most effort is required. Another part of his job is to actually push the machine from the rider's pits position to the pits' gate and then out on to the track in readiness for the rider to mount. If the Pit Marshal is chasing them, some quite chaotic conditions can some-times prevail as two or more pushers try to get their respective machines through the same space at the same time!
Silver, L. 'The Vital Cogs' in *The Speedway Annual* compiled by Silver, L. and Douglas, P. (London, Pelham Books, 1969)

Australian experience and know-how did much to help the fledgling sport of speedway develop in Britain. By the early 1930s, Britain was firmly established as the centre of world speedway. From the start of the 1930s, tracks drew crowds as big as those who turned out to watch football at White Hart Lane and Highbury. But unlike soccer crowds, speedway attracted a large number of women fans – at times, almost half the spectators were female. When the West Ham team rode away from home, a crowd of vivacious East London girls with scarves and rattles and crossed-hammer badges always supported them. This was because speedway was a relatively civilised form of sporting entertainment. Of course, the riders being young speed-devils – many of them handsome, often muscular, tanned Australians and Americans – was not a factor! However, history shows that tens of thousands of people of all ages came together in the stadium without a moment of unpleasantness.

The season that started in 1930 was West Ham's second of its three consecutive terms in the Southern League. Jimmy Baxter was still pulling the strings, although by that time he was under the auspices of West Ham Stadium Ltd. Having cashed in on the initial boom period, a number of the early stars of speedway had retired when the individual contests for appearance money gave way to team racing. Tiger Stevenson and Bluey Wilkinson were the only two team members from the previous season to start the new term with West Ham. Tommy Croombs, Arthur Westwood, Allen Kilfoyle, Bert Jones and Don Durrant were all new recruits.

The necessity of rebuilding the team took its toll and West Ham could go no higher than ninth position. Stamford Bridge put the Hammers out of the London Cup at the first hurdle, but West Ham managed to win the Essex County Championship, beating High Beech at Custom House and King's Oak and defeating Lea Bridge on West Ham dirt. Tiger Stevenson qualified for the Star Riders' Championship final as one of the League's top dozen scorers.

International speedway competition also got started in 1930, with the first Test series between England and Australia. Tiger Stevenson and Bluey Wilkinson were picked by their respective nations to ride in the third Test match at Stamford Bridge. Wilkinson was selected for a second time to ride in the fifth Test.

It was around this time that Stan Greening and speedway ace Wal Phillips designed the first speedway unit, largely by adapting a J.A. Prestwich (JAP) road-racing engine. It was so successful that it was to rule the dirt-tracks of Britain, Australia and the USA right through to the coming of the JAWA in the l960s. Wal was probably the first man to emerge as a 'master tuner'. A pre-war Stamford Bridge man, he first rode the engine he had put together in the summer of 1930. When it appeared, it swept all before it, making all other machines obsolete overnight.

Enter Hoskins

In 1931, the West Ham supporters were not attending in the numbers that they once had and this caused inevitable cash flow problems for Jimmy Baxter. An administrative change took place and Custom House Stadium was taken under the umbrella of Wembley Stadium Ltd. Arthur Elvin became promoter and Alec Jackson was appointed speedway manager.

However, the major impact on West Ham Speedway was the arrival of Johnnie Hoskins at Custom House. Hoskins, the founder of the speedway and entertainer supreme, realised that the public needed novel forms of motivation to attract them back to speedway's East End home. One of his first actions was to reduce the admission charge to 6d; no major speedway side could be watched for less. He went on to create a supporters' club, which had proved a successful strategy during his time at Wembley. At the start of April, nearly 500 people had paid 2s for membership. Each had received a claret and blue enamel badge and gained entitlement to admission to a range of social events that Hoskins arranged during the close season, so holding the supporter interest and income throughout the year, whilst connecting season to season. Fans in the club were also admitted to the enclosures for less than half the normal price. Occasionally, Hoskins was also able to broker reduced admission for supporters' club members at away tracks.

Tommy Croombs.

Stevenson, Wilkinson, Croombs and Kilfoyle maintained regular places in the West Ham side from the start of the 1931 timetable. Con Cantwell, Frank Randall, Reg and Cecil Bounds joined them. The former was to be among the highest League scorers of that term, and won the Essex Championship. He gained two Test caps in recognition of his achievements. He further justified his selection by scoring 10 points at Wembley in the third Test. Arthur Atkinson came to Custom House later in the season. Atkinson had learnt to ride a motorcycle at the age of thirteen. He had competed in grass-track and rough-riding races before taking to the cinders at Blackpool in 1928. The following year he was Yorkshire Champion and captain of Leeds. Arthur won the West Australian title that winter then joined Wembley in 1930, but a crash, which left him unconscious for three weeks, began a run of bad luck. He gradually regained his form on joining the Hammers in 1932, after a short time with York. Atkinson became a Test rider in 1936, making two Australian tours. In the latter part of his career, he took up farming.

Also making debuts at Custom House that year were Blos Bromfield, Tom Lougher and Morian Hansen, the calm and determined Dane. He was a big man for a speedway rider and one of the best European riders of the time. He made several visits to England before he joined West Ham in 1931, moving on to Hackney Wick when that club was formed in 1935. During the Australian speedway season of 1935/36, he broke his jaw in his first race, but did not let this interfere with his riding. In 1936, Morian Hansen wintered in England to qualify for a commercial pilot's license.

With Wilkinson and Croombs leading the charge, the West Ham team shot up the table, finishing the season in third place. This outcome was a marvellous achievement, especially as Stevenson played no part in things from the start of the year, missing over half the campaign, following a road accident. Croombs and Wilkinson qualified for the Star Riders' Championship final, with Croombs achieving a creditable third place. Croombs also gained selection for England in the Test series, appearing three times for his country. Reg Bounds was picked twice, notching up 10 points in the third Test at Wembley. Wilkinson rode in all five Test matches for Australia.

For the 1931 and 1932 seasons, both Jack and Norman Parker moved from Coventry to Southampton, where, in the absence of a signing-on fee (which was illegal at that time), they both received payment for 'painting the stands'. The 1933 season saw the brothers move again, this time to Clapton. The Clapton promotion only lasted one season before the whole team was moved to Harringay, where they remained until the outbreak of the Second World War. This is where and when the Parker boys began to make their mark on the tracks of Britain.

In 1932, West Ham also took part in the National Speedway Association Trophy, which was a league-style competition that preceded the National League Championship. It was the product of an amalgam between the Northern and Southern Leagues. At this time, West Ham had the basis of the team that was to serve the club for the next seven years. Ed 'Flash' Barker, who was also an accomplished wrestler, and Eric Chitty, a fair-haired Canadian, a successful singer, who often charmed the Custom House faithful with a tune of the day – broke into the side as did another Canadian Hammer, Jimmy Gibb (who had 'Never Gibb Up' tattooed on his chest).

West Ham skipper Stevenson, not wanting to repeat his enforced lay-off of the previous season, rode for several weeks with a broken collarbone, an injury he picked up at the start of the 1932 campaign, following a fall. The problem was only discovered after he collapsed in the pits a month or so after the incident. Small wonder he was known as 'Tiger'.

Eric Chitty, Arthur Atkinson, Ken Brett and Alec Mosely outside the West Ham workshops before the Second World War.

In the much stronger league, West Ham achieved sixth place. Wilkinson and Croombs again lead the Custom House pack. Croombs continued his habit of qualifying for the Star Riders' Championship final and took the Cundy Trophy.

JAP Domination

By 1932, the top men in speedway were opting for the JAP motorcycle, and they continued to do so for more than thirty years. Until 1966, all of speedway's World Champions gained their titles on JAP bikes, powered by engines basically the same as the JAP power plant of the early 1930s. Only the frames of the machines had changed drastically. In the late 1950s, Poland introduced the FIZ, but it failed to catch on, and it was not until Czechoslovakia came up with the JAWA-ESO that the JAP found itself facing a serious rival.

A Test Match At The Bridge

On the first Saturday in June 1932 at Stamford Bridge, England met Australia in front of 45,000 spectators. The England captain that day was Colin Watson of Wembley. Also in the side was Frank Varey. Frank was a great personality with huge affection for the fans, win or lose. As a mechanic, he took part in many motorcycle competitions before he started speedway racing in 1928. He never spared himself on the track and his sturdy constitution brought him through several bad injuries. His whirlwind riding in South America brought him the nickname 'The Red Devil'. He always rode for Belle Vue and was the original captain of the Manchester club.

Another Belle Vue man gaining a cap that day was Eric Langton, one of the world's greatest all-round motorcyclists. The Yorkshireman was a star almost from his first ride on the speedway. After captaining Leeds in 1929, he joined Belle Vue, leading the club to uninterrupted success from 1934. He went on to be a top scorer of the 1930s. In partnership with Jack Parker, he won many matches. Varey secured the British Championship in 1932 and won the League Riders' Championship in the same year. He was runner-up in 1934. Gaining second place in the 1936 World Championship was probably both the most glorious and the worst moment of his speedway career, having initially tied for first place.

Wally 'Nobby' Key was in the England line-up that day. At the time, he was with Crystal Palace and was one of the mainstays of that team for several seasons. He learnt the art of broadsiding on cinders at the Palace circuit in 1928 and went on to have short spells with Wembley, Cardiff and Nottingham. It was not until he returned to the Palace in 1931 that he became a truly top-class rider. With the Australian, Ron Johnson, he won a Best Pairs competition in 1934. When the Palace team transferred their headquarters and become known as New Cross, Key distinguished himself in many stylish rides on their new track.

Partnering Tom Farndon in this Test was George Greenwood, who had a glorious partnership with Harry Whitfield riding for Wembley in that club's best years. A Yorkshireman, George was winning Championships in the north at just seventeen years

Eric Chitty in action.

of age. He joined Wembley in 1929. In 1931, he rose from his sick bed to win all his races in Wembley's most difficult cup match of that term. Attached to Nottingham in 1933, he returned to Wembley in 1934, but sustained an arm injury. Again in Nottingham's colours, he won the Provincial League Riders' Championship in 1936 and came back to Wembley in 1937. After a spell with Hackney Wick, he took on the responsibility of captaincy at Nottingham.

The rest of the side was Wal Phillips (riding on his own track) and Arthur Warwick of the Bridge. The reserves were Syd Jackson of Coventry and Tommy Croombs of West Ham.

Australia fielded a very strong side, captained by the idol of the Bridge, Frank Arthur. The team included Dicky Case, of Wimbledon at the time. The fair-headed Queenslander was always cheerful, despite a number of injuries. Before speedway, he was employed on Queensland's railways. He did not achieve stardom until he joined Wimbledon in 1930, and it was in that year that he rode for Australian in the first Test ever held. He was to become a regular choice for his country. Case set a Test record when his partnership with Billy Lamont was unbeaten throughout the second match in 1932. Dicky was one of the most daring and determined riders and an exceptionally good captain, leading Coventry, Lea Bridge, Walthamstow and Hackney.

The Aussies also called on Wembley's Lionel Van Praag. He was a reserved and resolute rider, who was to become the first World Speedway Champion. Although he began his speedway career in 1926 and had ridden for his country since 1931, he did not reach his peak until 1936, when numerous successes culminated in his securing the

41

Ron Johnson, when captain of New Cross.

world title. First riding at Sydney, he came to Wembley in 1931 and went on to become club captain. A one-time typewriter mechanic, he developed into one of the best engineers in speedway, with a wonderfully equipped private workshop. He also had a great interest in flying.

Belle Vue hard man Max Grosskreutz was another Aussie on duty that day. Maximillian Octavius was the son of a Queensland farmer. He first took to the track at Brisbane and won the Australian Championship in 1928. After a year with Lea Bridge, he joined Belle Vue in 1930. He had a superlative Test record, riding in all 42 matches until mid-1936, when he suffered his only serious accident. Max retired at the end of that year with easily the highest ever score on the international scene (Australians or Englishmen). He went on to become a member of the Australian selection committee and manager of Norwich. He always rode with a characteristic, sweeping style. He was an exceptionally clever technician, and popularised the short-wheelbase machine.

The Australian side was completed by home star Jack Chapman, Dick Smythe, Wimbledon's Vic Huxley and Crystal Palace star Ron Johnson. The reserve pair looked very strong; they were West Ham's Bluey Wilkinson and Billy Lamont of Wimbledon.

As the riders paraded around the track, the atmosphere was electric. Heat one had the crowd on its toes from the start. Dicky Smythe fell on the first turn, only to have England's Colin Watson pile into the fence behind him. Up front, Arthur and Phillips were battling it out, with Frank coming out on top – England 2, Australia 3.

Ron Johnson won heat three for Australia, putting them into a three-point lead. In the following race, Australia were pushed right back by the superb riding of the English pair of Farndon and Greenwood. Tom took the lead from the start, but George did it the hard way by going around Van Praag on the last bend, giving England five race points, with just a single point going to Australia. This made the overall score England 12, Australia 11. More drama came in the next heat. Langton was shown the black flag and was left on the track. Varey shot ahead, winning from Smythe and Arthur.

A protest was lodged, as Langton had blocked Smythe. There were no starting gates at that time, riders going off by the green light. The re-run had just three riders: Varey of England, Smythe and Arthur of Australia. Smythe quickly took the lead and Varey had problems on the back straight, so this left the two Aussies in charge, but Smythe fell, leaving Frank Arthur the only finisher – Australia 14, England 12. Australia held the lead until heat seven when, once again, Greenwood and Farndon came out on top, taking maximum points. England 20, Australia 18.

By the interval, England still held on to that two-point lead. Australia replaced Smythe, as he had been injured in his previous ride. Bluey Wilkinson was the substitute. England pushed further ahead with a great ride from local star, Arthur Warwick.

Heat twelve saw Varey lead from the start, but Langton lost second place to a fighting Vic Huxley – England 37, Australia 31. In heat thirteen, Wilkinson failed to get his motor going, and Lamont was called in his place. Greenwood went straight into the lead only to lose his chain, before Aussie Frank Arthur fell at the first bend. This left Farndon to win with Lamont second. The next race saw Australia gain a 4-2 win through Case, with England's Wal Phillips second and Jack Chapman third.

In heat fifteen, Australia badly needed the points. Maxie Grosskreutz duly shot to the front and stayed there. Varey finished second with Langton third. Johnson fell on the third lap. By the last race, Australia needed a maximum score while England only wanted a point. The home side took the points, with Tom Farndon winning from Nobby Key. Australian star Vic Huxley was some ten lengths adrift and the final score was England 50, Australia 41.

England's scorers were: Colin Watson 8, Tom Farndon 11, George Greenwood 5, Wal Phillips 10, Frank Varey 8, Arthur Warwick 8, Tommy Croombs 0, Syd Jackson did not ride.

Australia's scorers were: Max Grosskreutz 7, Frank Arthur 6, D. Case 6, Vic Huxley 5, Bluey Wilkinson 5, Billy Lamont 4, Ron Johnson 4, Lionel Van Praag 2, Jack Chapman 2, Dick Smyth 0.

England went on to lose the second Test at Wembley 35-59, but gained revenge at Belle Vue, winning 53-43. The Aussies fought back to level the series at Crystal Palace, winning 49-45. The National Speedway Association decided to transfer the fifth Test from

The first ever Speedway World Champion, Lionel van Praag, 1936.

Southampton to Wembley to provide larger crowd capacity, owing to such public interest. On 15 September, England came out on top 51-42, winning the series. The National Speedway Association were proved right by having the largest ever speedway crowd, comparable to that of any football cup final. In heat seven, Vic Huxley equalled the track record of 78.4 seconds on a very heavy surface, and was to remain unbeaten throughout the match. West Ham's Bluey Wilkinson appeared in all five Tests for Australia, marking him out as a true international star.

Human Skill

There was yet another change of promotion at Custom House in 1933, when Fred Fearnley took over under the auspices of West Ham (1933) Ltd. The sad fact was that the sport was suffering a slow contraction because of the massive number of false starts taking place during meetings. The introduction of the starting gate helped the situation enormously, focusing the spectacle of speedway tighter on the racing and bringing in a new element of drama and, by way of starting technique, skill.

It is the skill involved in speedway that has always been its main attraction: the testing of human ability in contest. On the face of it, speedway is not as sophisticated as other forms of motorcycle racing. It is, basically, going down to the first bend and turning left. This vision of running round in circles has often been used by enthusiasts of other forms of motorised racing as an analogy to dismiss speedway, but it really does not do the sport justice. Dirt-surfaced tracks were (and are) harder to 'read' than paved surfaces. The speedway rider tended to produce two or even three racing 'grooves' – other motorcyclists riding on paved circuits usually create only a single racing line. Dirt tracks often changed dramatically during the course of a race or meeting, and a decent racing line early on might have been much less effective later in the proceedings. Learning to read a track and set machinery up to suit the prevailing conditions took considerable experience and expertise.

The speedway competitors often found themselves moving in a bunch at high speed. Negotiating the 'mobile chicanes' created by these conditions required a high degree of skill and compensated for the deficit of right-hand turns on a track.

Speedway bikes were not unsophisticated, but there has been generally less concern with technical development relative to other forms of motorcycle contest. The main objective in speedway was that the riders should compete against each other on equal terms, because the emphasis in the sport is very much on racing. In road competition, technical developments, inboard telemetry, fuel and tyre considerations and pit stops have ensured that the sport is less and less about driving and racing, and more and more about computer technology and design. This has taken the edge off racing in recent years.

Speedway on the other hand, despite its many shortcomings, has always been about real head-to-head, wheel-to-wheel racing. Its initial fascination for the public was that it put men on machines and they fought out a result, calling on their will, strength, physical power, racing instincts and ability. It was a true contest of the spirit, calling the higher human qualities of judgement and courage, whilst applying the reactions and

'Soiled in the smoke of war' – England v. *Australia,* c. *1949 – Vic Duggan, Lionel van Praag and Aub Lawson.*

intelligence of the rider. As such, the spectacle allowed people to go to the edge and others to witness their collective adventure and individual daring.

Panthers, Cheetahs And A Tiger

Johnnie Hoskins was a very useful person to have around in a crisis such as West Ham (and speedway in general) experienced in the mid-1930s. Hoskins, who, after his arrival at West Ham, was to sever his ties with Wembley, was an extremely popular character at Custom House. He became something of an icon in subsequent years and was still being visited by West Ham fans at his home in Canterbury in the early 1980s (he was ninety years old in April 1982).

Hoskins was a showman of the Barnam class. It should be remembered that the West Ham Speedway team rented the track from West Ham Stadium and, as such, the side couldn't rely on subsidies from stock-car or greyhound racing. To recreate interest in his team and pull crowds back to speedway, mostly at Tuesday evening meetings, Hoskins introduced cheetah racing to the Docklands (and almost certainly the world), advertising the appearance of the fastest animals on Earth in a race around the West Ham track. In a trial run in the morning, the big cats got loose in the stadium and the directors, fearing lawsuits and injuries, rebelled. But faith had to be kept, it was too late to cancel the event.

The race started before a tremendous crowd of curious people. After a run of thirty yards, the animals came to the end of their leather tethers and halted. Hoskins felt an apology was appropriate. He contritely announced:

– Ladies and gentlemen. Tonight we advertised five cheetahs, but in reality there are six...

Quick as a flash came a shout from the crowd:

– Yes, and we know who the sixth is.

This wasn't the end of Hoskins' dealings with big cats. He went on to organise a race between a speedway rider and a panther, the latter running on the greyhound track. Next, Hoskins turned his mind to camels, but after limited success in the 'dromedary stakes' (you couldn't get the brutes to run), Johnnie saw elephants as an answer to West Ham's problems. He thought they could always be relied on to swell the gates. How he reached this conclusion is a mystery, but he managed to find three elephants in the East End and get them delivered to Custom House. However, he was disappointed as they lacked the exotic trappings of the subcontinent, having no Indian Rajah mounted in style. He complained to the supplier, who responded in true cockney fashion:

– Cor Guvnor. What the 'ell do you expect for ten pounds, three elephants and a flippin' Rajah as well?

Three Australians – Max Grosskreutz, Aub Lawson and Vic Duggan.

Howdy Byford and Eric Chitty.

Hoskins pushed his luck to the limit, bringing in celebrities, film stars and radio person-alities, wild animals, glass coaches, circus ponies to celebrate weddings and bands, often accompanying 'a ditty from Eric Chitty'. Johnnie organised hoop races for 200 children at a time, and on one occasion employed a troupe of Russian horsemen – a few of which (both 'Russians' and horses) looked suspiciously 'local'. There seemed to be no end to the Hoskins imagination. He arranged a vast array of publicity stunts and interval entertainments in an ongoing struggle to make West Ham the most talked about team in the country and the best supported. Donkey derbies and firework displays, singing Cossacks, acrobats, exhibitions by the Everywoman's Health Movement and 'Amazing Feats by Dogs'. Speedway riders competed against horse and jockey, ice-skaters and greyhounds. At one mid-September meeting, between the heats of the semi-final of the London Cup against New Cross, Peter Dawson, the world famous Australian tenor, performed for the Custom House crowd.

Between dreaming up and sorting out stunts, the mercurial Hoskins was forever on the telephone to the steward. In the full gaze of the fans, he would lodge complaints and protests in an effort to wind the supporters up. During the interval, the riders would habitually burn his hat, having doused it liberally in methanol. When fully alight, they would play football with it.

Johnnie Hoskins also organised charity events in support of various local organisa-tions. On 7 October 1938, at the Grand Thanksgiving Meeting in aid of Queen Mary's Hospital for the East End, the following event was advertised in the 4d programme: Will Fyffe, famous Scots Comedian will present the Lord Mayor of London's Cup to the Winner of the Speedway Event, Grand Draft Horse Derby. Official starter Captain W.J. Neilson, M.C.

Horse	Jockey
Tishy	J. Hoskins
Nonsuch	Charlie Spinks
Charity	Eric Chitty
Stingy	Colin Watson
Liberal	Arthur Atkinson
Thanksalot	Phil Bishop

Atkinson rode home in first place, followed by Hoskins and Watson.

In 1939, Hoskins managed to organise the first royal patronage of speedway when the Duchess of Kent attended a charity meeting at Custom House. Visitors to the home of West Ham Speedway also included the Lord Mayor of London and Prince Philip. There seemed to be no end to Johnnie's enterprise or connections. He appeared to know the Canning Town residents who were keeping wild animals – such as elephants and camels – in their back yards for rent and people who knew people who were in cahoots with the upper echelons of the Royal family! Hoskins was a phenomenon in himself, well suited to the West Ham area, which has always loved the person ready to fight their corner and the individual prepared to 'have a tin bath (laugh)'.

Tiger, Tiger Burning Bright …

Free from injury, the fans began to see the true potential of Tiger Stevenson for the first time. Alongside Wilkinson and Croombs, he became one of the West Ham elite riders – a group of the very highest quality. West Ham's strength was reflected in the League table as they finished third, a single point separating them from Wimbledon in second place.

Following a season of records being broken around the tracks of Britain, Stevenson was eventually nominated to race Ron Johnson for the British Match Race Championship of 1933. Although born in Scotland, Johnson moved to Perth, Western Australia, taking on the work of a lumberman when he left school. He came to England in 1928 and, after a short spell at Salford under Johnnie Hoskins, he signed

An advertisement for Eric Chitty's sports shop.

Left: *King of the Crash No. 1 and West Ham immortal – Phil Bishop.* Right: *Arthur Atkinson, pre-Second World War international. After the war he became a promoter at Custom House and then took up riding again, having spells with West Ham and Harringay.*

for Crystal Palace (who, in 1934, became New Cross). Johnson was very light, but exceptionally strong – he had also been a good amateur boxer. Not always having the best of luck, his speedway career cost him some toes and fingers. Johnson was recognised as a scientific racer, using logic and tactical acumen to enhance his riding. He reached something of a peak in 1933. The following year, he was to make the highest score in the Test series, riding for his adopted country.

Stevenson won both legs of the British Match Race Championship and became one of the few Londoners to reach star class. Wilkinson and Croombs made the Star Riders' final. This was being run under a new format in 1933, allowing two members from each League team to compete at Wembley. Wilkinson fought his way to the Championship-deciding run-off, which also included two riders from Crystal Palace: Tom Farndon and Ron Johnson. The first half of the race saw Wilkinson and Farndon locked together in mortal combat, but it was Farndon's day. Wilkinson's front tyre went adrift and Farndon cut loose. Johnson also zoomed passed him. The Aussie Hammer had to live with third place.

Recognition of Stevenson's achievements for the season came when he was made captain of England for four of that year's Test matches, leading his country to a 3-2 series victory and scoring double figures in all the matches in which he rode. This was Stevenson's great year. Once more, Bluey Wilkinson appeared in all five Tests for Australia and he too made double figures in four of them, making the Aussie's highest score in the process.

3

CLARET AND BLUES

Referee's Box
Whilst it is called a 'Box' this is really a small room which must be situated either directly in line or almost in line with the starting tapes, so that the referee gets a clear and unobstructed view of the whole track. It is from this box that all the electrical equipment is operated and there is a panel of switches in front of the referee whilst he works. This box must also be connected by telephone to the starting line, and to the pit area, as well as to the announcer so that the referee can keep him in constant touch with changes etc., which team managers may make. Also, so that he can inform the announcer of the official race results, times, etc. The time keeper usually sits in the same box as the referee and in some cases the announcer does also.
Silver, L. 'Anatomy of a Speedway' in *The Speedway Annual* compiled by Silver, L. and Douglas, P. (London, Pelham Books, 1969)

Perhaps the most bizarre track event staged at West Ham was The Pork Stakes. This was a pig race, complete with 'height-challenged' jockeys. The one-lap event, whilst not a complete success, did have some credibility as a contest. Two of the riders were long-time rivals within the swine racing fraternity that was apparently something just less than an obscure, fringe distraction between the wars. Indeed, 'Tiny' Ted Peace and Jack 'Swiper' Budge, despite being small in stature, were giants in the pig-racing world.

For the Custom House event, Peace rode a fine-looking dappled sow known as 'Delighted Maude'. She was said to be a champion of sorts and in her racing colours looked very tasty. Budge's mount was 'Harry the Wag'. He came to the line snorting angrily, and his pilot seemed to be having trouble holding the attention of the disgruntled beast. It was a wonderful sight: the noble steeds champing at the bit, their jockeys robed in the appropriate livery – which featured the colours of their sponsors (Maude was bedecked in the blue and white of Penn's, the bespoke butchers, and Harry in the green and black of Walker's, greengrocer to the gentry). These emporia were based in the Barking Road, next door to one another, so the rivalry was built in from before the off.

As the tapes went up, two of the eight or so runners squealed in horror and took their bewildered passengers off into the stands. However, the bulk of the field made for the first bend with an admirable competitive attitude. Coming into the first straight, although one animal seemed to have expired, the pack was jostling for position at a furious pace. It wasn't until the last turn that Maude and Harry broke, showing themselves to be the thoroughbreds that they were. As they came into the home straight together, Peace and Budge were taking more cracks at each other with their whips than they were handing out to their mounts, but the crowd were up and cheering the brave porkers home.

As they neared the final glory, Maude struck for the line, but as she moved in front of Harry, in a fit of frustration and lust, The Wag leapt, like the great bull-boar he was, on the sow's rear, throwing the wretched Budge into the air. Peace, in blind panic, was now thrashing away at Harry with his little yet furious fists and whip, but to no avail. The pig was numbed to pain by his passion and in his hefty lurchings rammed his large head into Peace's back, sending him tumbling over the top of the now engrossed – if not altogether delighted – Maude. Budge, having recovered his feet, took advantage of Peace's perpendicular state. Rushing to the spot where he lay, Budge began to kick the prostrate Peace with gusto. As all this was going on, the chasing group had made up ground, but as they past the fighters and the lovers, Maude's racing instincts returned and she galloped on, apparently saddled by Harry, who, ever the wag, 'twinkle-toed' on his back legs behind her. Reaching the line before all her rivals, Maude was proclaimed the winner and bedecked in the victor's laurels. The stadium stood to applaud the champion and the whole sordid but entertaining affair.

When Budge and Peace were finally separated, there were a further arguments about the prize money and objections from other entrants about the winner's lack of a human jockey at the finish. However, it all came to naught and Maude became the stuff of legend – and maybe a few bacon sandwiches.

On a more serious level, the last Test of the 1933 season was held at West Ham and attracted a crowd of 82,400 – although some said it was closer to 100,000 as Custom House always had its share of 'stowaways'. One fan recalled: 'When I was a boy my granddad was a car park attendant at the track … he would let me and my mates in through a back way so we could watch free'. Another admitted that: 'I used to bunk in after the first race. I went to school with a girl whose dad sold the Percy Dalton peanuts. He used to open the gate for me.'

It was also not unusual for turnstile operators to let in 'two-for-one', especially in times of high unemployment. However many unofficial extras there were in the crowd, it was still a record attendance for both speedway and the stadium. Anyone who remembers those days will recall first the trams, then the trolley buses and double-decker diesels rolling from Plaistow underground station and the Greengate to Custom House crammed to the gunnels. There was never a better time for speedway in the East End.

Stanley Greening joined Fred Fearnley at Custom House in 1934 and as a team they co-promoted the Hammers. West Ham fielded a side in the Reserve League, or Second Division as it was sometimes referred to, as well as the National League.

The mighty trio of Stevenson, Wilkinson and Croombs started 1934 where they had left off in 1933. Arthur Atkinson, Eric Gregory, Arthur Warwick and Broncho Dixon all

Arthur Atkinson.

played useful supporting roles. Dixon won his debut race for West Ham, defeating Claude Rye of Wimbledon. Rye, a young South London motor salesperson before joining Wimbledon, had been one of the outstanding riders of the previous season, and became the first to reach a century of League points in that year. Shortly after achieving that distinction, however, his brilliant feats were unfortunately checked by a leg fracture, which he sustained on his Test debut. Subsequent injuries kept him out of the saddle, but brave perseverance earned him the reward of being appointed skipper of Wimbledon in 1937.

Stevenson just managed to pip Wilkinson as top scorer for the year; Croombs was a close third. Belle Vue and Wembley were dominant in the League and head and shoulders above their rivals. West Ham were content with fourth place at the completion of the fixture list. The Hammers did, however, beat Wembley in the last four of the London Cup. It was a close-run affair, but West Ham did well as they were without their skipper, Stevenson, who missed the match through injury. Stan Dell, who came into the side from the reserve team as a replacement for the inimitable Tiger, shocked many people who knew little of his potential in the first leg at New Cross by scoring 10 paid 11 from six rides.

The 'paid' or 'bonus' points system had been brought in to encourage team racing. Riders were paid for starting a race and received money for the points they scored. For example, in the 1950s at West Ham, Reg Fearman would be paid 35s per start and £2 for every point he scored. This potentially meant that a race would be an 'all against all' affair, with riders from the same side having everything to gain from 'running over' their team-mates. The 'points paid' system prevented this from happening in that if a partnership finished first and second, the runner-up would receive his two points, but get paid for the three points that had been awarded to his partner (score 2 paid 3). So it was possible, for instance, to ride in six races, come last in all of them, but receive payment for 18 points, if one's race partner had won all half-dozen contests: scored 0 paid 18. This meant that riders from the same team would help one another out. A West Ham rider might concentrate on blocking a Hackney man in third place rather than attempt to take the lead from his fellow Hammer and, at the same time, allow the

Hackney rider a 'free shot' at his claret and blue compatriot, thus risking the loss of team points. The 'paid' points would not go towards the match score, but they would be used in the calculations that established a rider's average on which team selection was decided as they expressed his skill as a team rider.

The final of the London Cup pitted the Hammers against New Cross, but the East Londoners were desperately unlucky and just missed out on victory. However, West Ham did win the Junior League without losing a single match. The West Ham side included Ken Brett, Rol Stobart, Stan Dell and Wal Morton.

Bluey Wilkinson and Tommy Croombs were again the Hammers' representatives at the Star Riders' final. Wilkinson was not able to replicate his success of the previous year and neither of the West Ham riders got through to the run-off. Tiger Stevenson had had his Match Race title taken from him by Vic Huxley at the start of the season, but he was to ride in three Tests for England. Croombs was also selected three times during the series. Now, as usual, Wilkinson was a fixture in the Australian side for all five Tests. He twice made double figures and was top of the scorers in the last Test at Custom House, making a total of 16 points.

A Test At Wembley

The Test at the Empire Stadium, Wembley saw Australian Ron Johnson take on the mighty partnership of Gordon Byers and Ginger Lees. Byers was riding motorcycles in his native Sunderland at the age of fourteen, but learnt his profession at Middlesborough in 1929. Later, he rode for Newcastle and was a leading member of the Leeds team in 1931. Gordon reached his peak when he joined Wembley in 1932, where he began the high-scoring pairing with Ginger Lees; at the age of nineteen, he won the club's championship and became England's youngest Test rider. Byers was to be picked for England again over the next two years, before a leg injury and eye trouble caused by cinder dust set him back. Although he came back in 1936, he was forced to retire a year later.

Harold Riley Lees – a Lancastrian nicknamed 'Ginger' – was the first rider to success-fully adopt the foot-forward style that was in general use by the late 1930s. Lees was a famous motorcycle trails rider and racer before he went on to the speedways in 1928. He started with White City (Manchester) moving on to Burnley. He joined Liverpool before going to Preston and, in 1932, he signed for Wembley. Lees was a regular English Test rider from 1931 onwards and headed the list of English riders at the end of 1934. He retired after breaking a leg in 1935, but returned to the cinder fray when his club was short-handed.

Lees and Byers quickly took the lead from Bluey Wilkinson. After nearly a lap, Ron Johnson was on their tails, trying everything he knew. It was impossible to either run round his foes or to go inside them with Lees there; the only way was between them. However, every time Johnson tried it, the Englishmen 'closed the gate' on him. Ron was determined, however, and spurred on by the sight of the yellow flag, he used every ounce of steam down the straight to drive between the pair as they shot off for the bend. Johnson knew that the slightest waver would result in him touching one or the other of his opponents, but his nerve was rock steady, and his machine control wonderful.

Lees immediately opened out again and drifted, managing to hang on to a bare lead, but Byers was beaten and the famous partnership was split. A more hazardous piece of riding more cleverly executed would be impossible. The crowd got to its feet and roared its appreciation. Total strangers slapped one another on the back and strained their voices to the limits. Everyone knew that they had seen a truly exceptional sporting performance – skilled precision mixed with bravery and born out of a creative imagination – speedway, sport and life at its best.

From Hope To Disaster

Another change on the management side in 1935 saw Johnnie Hoskins and Victor Martin link up as co-promoters of the Hammers. At this time, the West Ham supporters' club had a membership of 14,277. Throughout the country there were about 70,000 speedway supporters' club members. West Ham finished the season in third place in the League and again reached the final of the London Cup, but also again, they lost, this time to Harringay.

Arthur Atkinson, Arthur Warwick and Broncho Dixon (who was one of the first northern riders to visit the south) continued to ably support the Hammers' 'holy trinity'. Jack Dixon had astonished London speedway fans by his hectic riding in 1929. By the mid-1930s, he was a reliable member of the West Ham team, but he was still known by his early nickname of 'Broncho'. A star almost from his first ride at

Aub Lawson, after he converted to a 'foot-forward' rider in 1948

Middlesborough, he turned out for Stamford Bridge, Sheffield, Belle Vue, Wembley and Hackney, before he settled down with West Ham. Jack was also popular in Copenhagen, where he often rode. During his racing career, he suffered numerous crashes and lost the tops of two of his fingers.

West Ham's development policy was paying off, with Stan Dell, Ken Brett and Rol Stobart, all members of the junior side of 1934, achieving promotion to the senior team.

The format of the Star Riders' Championship was changed dramatically in 1935. Each track staged a qualifying round, culminating in a sixteen-rider Wembley final that would be decided over twenty heats. Each finalist met every other competitor once in four-man races (previously, the heats had been three-rider affairs). With the restrictions of club representation further relaxed, Wilkinson, Croombs and Stevenson all got to the final. Wilkinson finished equal fourth, Croombs made ninth place whilst Stevenson could do no better than equal eleventh.

It is hard to describe the comradeship that existed between riders before the Second World War and throughout the 1950s, particularly in an age where sport has raised its professional class to a level that leaves them out of touch with those who, literally, support them. Speedway riders, supporters, and those who worked to make meetings possible were a close fraternity. The competitions of the dirt oval, much more than other mass spectator sports of the time – for example, soccer and cricket – were a community affair. Maybe it was its 'life and death' scale that made speedway like this. People in the crowd felt the hurt, the pain and the triumph of the riders, whilst the men who rode the bikes sensed this compassion. Perhaps this instance will help demonstrate the nature of this empathic atmosphere: Tommy Croombs and Ken Brett were often riding partners for West Ham. On a racing night at Hackney Wick, they were paired against the Wick's Dusty Haigh and Bristolian Bill Clibbett. Both these 'men of the marsh' had hot reputations. Clibbett had ridden for numerous clubs. He had made a name for himself at Harringay and on moving to Wimbledon he paired up with another Westcountry man, Len Parker. This partnership was a huge success. Clibbett took on the captain's role at Plymouth from 1932 to 1934, before joining Hackney in 1935.

As the four combatants roared into the first lap, the usual excitement of a local derby was heightened by the prospect of an well-balanced encounter. However, after an early struggle, the heat was brought to a premature end when all four riders crashed together. When the fog of exhaust fumes and shale dust had cleared, a heap of flesh and still-groaning machines was revealed. A veil of silence fell on the track. Three of the riders staggered to their feet, but one was left, unmoving on the dirt. Dusty Haigh had blood streaming from his nose and ears. He was dead when he was lifted from the track. No announcement was made and the meeting went on, but everyone guessed the worst and what remained of the event was a sombre affair. Clibbert never really got over this tragedy. A hernia held him back until 1937, but he was never to fulfil the potential he had shown before that sad night. A lover of the country, he spent a great deal of time shooting and fishing.

'Mr Australia' Bluey Wilkinson again rode in all five Test matches of 1935. Croombs was selected for four Tests, including one held at Custom House where he was the top English scorer. Tiger Stevenson was restricted to just one international appearance.

A second team, known as West Ham Hawks, competed in the National Provincial Trophy in 1936, riding their home matches at Southampton. This year was to be a disastrous one for the Hammers: the side ended their season by propping up the entire League. Throughout the campaign, Hoskins sought to revive his side by the infusion of new blood. The previous season's squad, which had been a mixture of experience and youth, was reinforced by Mick Murphy, who though born in Perth, Western Australia, was thought to be typical example of an Irish rider – always cheerful, he gave the impression that he was unaffected by his lack of luck, which included breaking a leg on three occasions. Murphy's real name was John Glass (illustrating exactly what there is in a name). He had three years' experience on Australian tracks before joining Stamford Bridge in 1931. He was outstanding for Plymouth in 1933 and 1934. He then moved to Hackney, before joining the set-up at Custom House. He was to move on to New Cross in 1937. Murphy was in Australia during the winter of 1936/37, involved mainly in track management, but still found time to win the West Australian Championship. He gained a number of Test caps throughout his roving and varied career.

The 'King of Crashes', Phil Bishop, also came into the West Ham team at this time. He exemplified the type of attitude Hoskins nurtured throughout his reign at West Ham, which was distinguished by good humour, informality and conviviality. He fostered the kind of community relationship that would never be repeated in speedway. His team had a way of making friends and bringing entertainment with them, along with daring and sporting endeavour. For example, at Southampton one night the tall, elegant promoter of Harringay, Tom Bradbury Pratt, appeared at the starting line adorned in full evening attire, ready for a late night appointment. Phil Bishop, by this time a popular rider at Custom House and around the tracks in general, appeared before the crowd with a bucket of water and approached innocently enough to exchange a greeting. Suddenly, four gallons of cold water cascaded down the starched white front of the elegantly dressed director. Although Pratt nearly had a heart attack, riders and fans were in hysterics. Few of speedway's executive class were to tempt Bishop in this way again.

Phil Bishop, with what became the West Ham spirit, combined a light-hearted approach with fine performance skill. Bishop learnt the broadside at Lea Bridge but he first came to prominence in 1930, as the star of the High Beech side, and was almost unconquerable on his own track. He was one of the few men to defeat Vic Huxley that year. From High Beech he went to Southampton, Clapton and Harringay (where he was a successful partner to Jack Ormston, the dapper northerner who started riding at Middlesborough in 1929). Ormston, who was to become captain of Wembley, won the London Championship in 1930 and was selected to ride for England in the very first Test series that took place that year. He rode well enough to win a second cap in that initial series and a third the following year. His international career continued in 1932 with two more appearances for England. Ormston was also a member of the Wembley

Phil Bishop hammerin' round in 1949.

side that won the League three times, took the National Cup twice and, on two occasions were victorious in the London Cup. He retired in 1933, but came back to help Birmingham in 1934 and firmly re-established himself when he joined Harringay in 1935.

West Ham was to be Phil Bishop's last club. His eagerness was often his undoing: he had over 400 crashes and escaped few League campaigns without injury. At the end of the 1936 season, Phil fell and broke his leg. He later lost his life in a motor accident, together with several of his rider friends, when travelling in Belgium.

The Hammers had also opened their doors to a young Canadian called Eric Chitty. He trained as an electrician in his hometown of Toronto, and he rode as an amateur in motorcycle hill-climbs, trials and dirt-track races from 1928; he was just nineteen at the time. Eric was immensely successful in 1930, when he was runner-up in the Canadian Championship. He retired through illness for two years, but in 1933 he turned professional in the USA. He was injured in 1934, but concluded the season by becoming Canadian Champion. In the 1935 Eastern US Championship, he did well to take third place. This encouraged him to chance his arm in England, where he arrived with no more than ten shillings to his name. Johnnie Hoskins was quick to sign him up. In his first days with West Ham, Chitty looked awkward and just couldn't get used to the English tracks. After eleven outings he had brought his side the paltry total of 15 points. He was dropped from the team, but Hoskins remembered that Bluey Wilkinson had shown a similar lack of aptitude when he first took to the Custom House oval and, despite having both Croombs and Stevenson out injured for most of the season, Hoskins held on to his Toronto prodigy.

Tommy Croombs always hugged the inside edge of the track whenever possible; he was a talented rider, but unlucky with injuries. The team never really recovered from having him and the Tiger out at the same time. At the end of the year, Hoskins, even using disaster to promote the club, sent miniature wooden spoons to every member of the Supporters' Club. It was typical of the fans that these become very much sought after in subsequent years.

It was also around this time that manufacturers were looking to develop the speedway bike. For example, experiments were being undertaken with the 'CAC' Harley Davidson 500cc engine. Basically, this was a copy of the English four-stud JAP motor that dominated speedway during the 1930s. It was developed and ridden by Harley factory rider Joe Petrali in an attempt to surpass the JAP. However, the engine failed to do well and only twenty were ever made. A small lever on the lower right side of the engine manually opened the exhaust valve during starting.

4
GOLDEN AGE ON A WORLD STAGE

Rakers

These four men are really assistants to the starting marshal, and they are merely there to help in general, assisting the riders to get into their proper gate position, and perhaps helping to re-start a machine that has stalled on the line. One of them usually has the job of handing the appropriate flag to the starting marshal at the correct time. Some tracks do not employ these men at all, and they are not as essential as other staff, but they certainly add to the efficiency of running the meeting. One of their jobs is to pull the starting gate tapes down on to the magnets ready for the 'Off'; if they were not present, the starting marshal would have that job added to his already over-crowded list. Probably the most important part of their job is to rake back into the starting area the shale thrown out by the riders' rear wheels as they roar off at the rising of the tapes. Again, the starting marshal would have to try to cope with this job as well, if these men were absent. Of course, some tracks employ less than four men on this job, and often two men can cope very efficiently.
Silver, L. 'The Vital Cogs' in *The Speedway Annual* compiled by Silver, L. and Douglas, P. (London, Pelham Books, 1969)

The inaugural World Championship was held at Wembley and it was to become the most important event in the speedway calendar. Australian Lionel Van Praag won the first world title. The prize money for that first event was £500 for first place, £250 for the runner-up and £100 for the third rider over the line. This was big money in 1936. The tournament was another brainchild of Johnnie Hoskins' and was part of an effort to spread the speedway word farther afield. Efforts had been made to introduce speedway to Germany and Scandinavians had already adopted it, quickly producing a top-class rider in Morian Hansen of Denmark. Sweden, for a time, banned the sport on the grounds that it was too dangerous – an ironic move in view of Sweden's domination of the sport in later years.

Places as far apart as South America and Egypt saw speedway, while North America produced successors to Sprouts Elder in the form of Wilbur Lamoreaux and the Milne brothers, Jack and Cordy. The latter was the younger. He came to Hackney Wick in 1936 when the club was short-handed. His steady riding went a long way towards the Wick's success in that period. The Milnes were Californians, hailing from Pasadena, USA. Cordy first rode speedway in 1931 at a Californian meeting. He won the USA national title in 1933 and 1935. A successful tour in Australia preceded his arrival in England. He was also a great golfer and took full advantage of the British courses.

Jack Milne became an instant success when he joined New Cross in 1936. Jack started racing in his home town in 1932; three years later he was joint runner-up in the USA Championship. He was one of the outstanding riders in the 1935/36 Australian season. In 1936 he lost his left thumb in a crash at West Ham, but went on to qualify for the World Championship final. A white-liner and a very reliable rider, Jack Milne's form at the start of the 1937 season was better than ever. He won the London Riders' Championship at New Cross on 30 June 1937.

Right from the start, the World Final pulled the best out of the qualifying riders. Frank Charles, the Wembley rider, smashed the track record in the final, tying for fourth place overall with Cordy Milne. Charles had made one of the greatest comebacks of all time. Following early success with Sheffield, White City (Manchester), Leeds and the English Test team, he disappeared from the limelight. Then in 1933, when a Belle Vue reserve, he won the Wembley Championship and broke the track record. He was transferred to Wembley in 1935, where he was almost unbeatable and won the League Riders' Championship. He made the best score of the 1936 Test series and became the only rider to go through eighteen Test heats undefeated.

West Ham, 1937. From left to right: Eric Chitty, Tommy Croombs, Arthur Atkinson, Phil Bishop, Johnnie Hoskins (promoter), Alec Moseley (mechanic), Broncho Dixon, Bluey Wilkinson, Charlie Spinks and Tiger Stevenson on the bike.

For all its international flavour, in the early years the World Championship only attracted riders based in Britain. Not that it mattered much – before and immediately after the Second World War, any speedway rider of talent was competing on British tracks.

The 1936, 1937 and 1938 tournaments consisted of a series of British qualifying rounds in which the riders picked up bonus points. The sixteen top scorers qualified for the final and the bonus points were added to the score each rider made in the final. Bonus points were to be a crucial factor in deciding the outcome. Bluey Wilkinson qualified for the first ever World Championship final with 10 bonus points, just 3 behind Belle Vue's Eric Langton and 2 behind Wembley's Lionel Van Praag. At Wembley, Wilkinson won every race. In any final after the war, he would have been the World Champion. He scored a 15-point maximum, but failed to win the tournament because he had scored fewer bonus points than Lionel Van Praag. As in the 1933 Star Riders' final, Bluey had to be content with third place.

Another West Ham rider, Arthur Atkinson, also qualified for the final but walked away a little disappointed with his fifteenth place.

For the sixth consecutive year, Wilkinson was selected for the Australia Test side in all five matches of the series. No other rider taking part in the contest could equal this feat. He ranked number three among Australian scorers up to end of 1936. He also made the second best Australian score in the series, matching his achievement of 1935. Atkinson and Croombs were selected for the England side when the series came to Custom House. After a career of success, the great Vic Huxley returned to Australia in October 1936 and announced his retirement early in 1937, having bought a business in his native land.

Hammers Champions

Johnnie Hoskins played on his instincts and took a risk, giving Eric Chitty another chance at the start of the 1937 season. As was usual for Hoskins, his gamble paid off. More or less keeping faith with the men that had finished at the foot of the table in 1936, West Ham turned the form book on its head, taking the League title with a swagger and a great deal of panache, winning all but half-a-dozen matches out of twenty-four contests. This ended the Mancunian domination of the sport, preventing Belle Vue from achieving an historic fifth successive championship. The smell of 'dope' was never more fragrant in the air around Custom House.

Hoskins explained that the success was founded on 'a heart full of hope and a hat full of hooey!' Which, at the time, sounded good but probably meant very little. The success was perhaps more to do with Arthur Atkinson and Eric Chitty finding their feet and competing more effectively alongside the big three of the Hammers side. The West Ham team at this point had a handful of international-class riders. By the end of the season, Chitty was number two only to Wilkinson, averaging 9.37. In his last 6 meetings away from Custom House he amassed a total of a paid 56 points. Wilkinson began the season like a rocket, dropping just 3 points in his first eight matches. However, a broken collarbone put an end to his impressive scoring tally and also put him out of the World Championship. Nevertheless, Bluey still managed to finish the season with an average of 10.13, and an overall fourth place in the riders' table, five places above his fellow Hammer, Chitty. Tommy Croombs made eleventh in the table and Atkinson took thirteenth spot. Stevenson came in at twenty-first. The other two regular members of the team, Charlie Spinks and Broncho Dixon, were in twenty-eighth and twenty-ninth position respectively. That meant that the Hammers had two riders in the top ten, four in the best twenty and seven of the leading thirty men in the League. This explains, much more clearly than the theory put forward by Hoskins, why the East London side had dominated the League in 1937.

The claret and blue was not so dominant in cup situations, however. Hackney Wick beat West Ham in the first round of the National Trophy, whilst New Cross defeated the Hammers in both legs of the final of the London Cup.

With Wilkinson absent from the World Championship final, Eric Chitty took up the West Ham cause on the world stage. Unfortunately, he did not replicate his League form and finished in equal eleventh place. Atkinson made thirteenth. Tommy Croombs finished at the foot of the list of finalists; ironically, one of his two points was gained by defeating Lionel Van Praag, the reigning champion.

1937 was to be the USA's big year in the World Championships. Americans took first, second and third places (the first time one nation had monopolised the tractor ride). Jack Milne won from Wilbur Lamoreaux and Cordy Milne.

Wilkinson was, almost inevitably, in the Australian side for the single Test of that year. But injury ruled him out of selection for the first two Overseas teams. He was top-scorer in the Test match, bagging 17 points. Arthur Atkinson also rode in that contest, scoring 12, which was enough to get him two more caps. Tommy Croombs rode once for his country, whilst Eric Chitty turned out for the Overseas team three times. Spinks got a single ride for what was a magnificent international side.

Following the achievements of the West Ham team in 1937, the membership of the Supporters' Club climbed to something near the 40,000 mark. West Ham Hawks (the Hammers' reserve team) again operated in 1938, riding their home National League Division Two fixtures at Dagenham.

Severe injuries to Tiger Stevenson and Eric Chitty curtailed any West Ham ambition to hold on to the Championship. However, they were superb in the circumstances, finishing in second place to New Cross, the team run by Hoskins' deadly rival, Fred Mockford. It was Mockford who dubbed Hoskins the Admiral of Barking Creek. Hoskins countered by calling Fred the New Cross Newt.

Eric Chitty turned out for just eight matches before he was injured, although in that time he was able to win the London Riders' Championship – much to the chagrin of the moribund Mockford – at the vipers' nest of New Cross, becoming the first West Ham rider to achieve this distinction. Stevenson was crocked in July having suffered concussion and serious head injuries at Wembley. However, even without these calamitous injuries, it is doubtful if the Hammers would have held on to their title. With the exception of Bluey Wilkinson, the seasonal averages of each team member declined. For instance, Tommy Croombs' total deteriorated from 8.92 to 7.88 and Dixon's slumped from 5.91 to 4.69. This apart, at the time of Stevenson's accident, his average had dropped by more than 1.5 points. Atkinson was ranked number two at Custom House for the first time, but Wilkinson rode better than at any time in his career. Bluey had a fantastic season. His average improved to 10.63, placing him in the number three spot in the League. In the final nine matches of the term, he dropped just 4 points. He won a cabinet full of trophies, including the Tom Stenner Cup, the Daily Sketch and the Knight of Speed trophies and the Tom Farndon Memorial Trophy.

In the Test series against England, Wilkinson rode in all five matches, never failing to be top-scorer. He record a marvellous sum of 80 points – establishing a new Test record that was to remain unbeaten in the history of the Australia/England contests. In a total of 38 Test appearances, Wilkinson scored 359 points (nearly 9.5 points per outing). However, it was the World Championship that was to be the flame-haired Aussie power-house's supreme triumph, although it was a victory he came near to missing.

5

BLUEY WILKINSON, HAMMER OF WEMBLEY

Public Accommodation

Of course every speedway track must have accommodation for the public so that it can exist at all! The quality of this accommodation is usually dictated by existing conditions within the stadium when the speedway is installed. There are tracks of course which have to be converted into speedway stadiums and in which the public accommodation has been altered and improved to suit the sport. An example of this may be seen at Kings Lynn where the promoter leased a derelict greyhound stadium and converted it for the motor-cycle sport and over a period of time has made it more and more comfortable for the public. What is most desirable of course is covered accommodation with seating not too far from the safety fence so that the atmosphere and noise can be enjoyed by the spectators whilst they are out of reach of what the English weather can dish out. Most stadiums have some accommodation of this kind and some plain terracing where the public can stand in the open to watch the racing. Strangely enough many members of the public seem to prefer standing on the terraces to sitting in a grandstand and it must be said that speedway can be enjoyed just as much in what may seem in some instances, primitive conditions as in the most luxurious grandstand.

Silver, L. 'Anatomy of a Speedway' in The Speedway Annual compiled by Silver, L. and Douglas, P. (London, Pelham Books, 1969)

The bonus points system continued to divide the speedway, but there were some alterations in procedure for the 1938 season. Changes were also made to the method of qualification for the World Championship, with fifty-six riders from the Second Division battling it out in preliminary rounds. The best six performers from this group progressed to the first round proper that included forty-two First Division qualifiers. Half of these men then moved forward to a championship round. This produced sixteen top-scoring riders who contested the final at Wembley on 1 September. Bonus points were calculated only on the championship round, which reduced the divide between the top and bottom scorers of the bonuses.

Bluey Wilkinson was going to leave nothing to chance following the pain the bonus points system had given him two years before. He had no less than 53 qualifying points, giving him the top bonus of 8 points under the complicated system used in 1938. But, two of the strongest competitors in the final, Jack Milne and Wilbur Lamoreaux, had 7 points each, so Bluey would still need to perform at his best.

Wembley saw 93,000 fans turn up for the confrontation, despite the news that some of the best qualifiers might not be able to compete. Lionel Van Praag had a leg injury, Jack Milne was down with 'flu and the evening before the final, Wilkinson was involved in a bad crash in the final of scratch race at New Cross. This was the same event that three years before had claimed the life of Tom Farndon (on the evening before the Star Championship). Wilkinson had ridden in that tragic event and the memory must have concentrated his mind. Bluey thought he had broken his collarbone, as he was unable to move his arm, but he refused to have it x-rayed for fear that it would mean his preclusion from the World Final. The next morning he went to White Hart Lane, the home of Tottenham Hotspur Football Club, for special treatment. He needed the help of fellow Aussies Clem Mitchell and Len Stewart to get to Wembley that evening. When he arrived at the twin towers, Bluey was barely able grip the throttle and was unable to raise his arm to shoulder level. His left leg was also injured, to the extent that he needed to be lifted on to his bike for each ride. It was to be a night of pain for Wilkinson.

Adding to Bluey's problems, both Lamoreaux and Jack Milne were back on their feet. As if all this wasn't enough, Wilkinson's draw obliged him to contest successive races – heats four and five – and to compete against the two favourites for the title: the 1936 victor, Van Praag, and the 1937 runner-up, Lamoreaux, in the second of those heats.

Van Praag, Lamoreaux and Jack Milne each won their first race. Wilkinson then had to ride in his consecutive heats. Bluey was able to summon all his racing guile and riding strength to win both races in two of the fastest times of the night. He also won his next two heats and then lined up for heat nineteen against the reigning global champion, Jack Milne. The American had dropped but a single point, to Lamoreaux in heat ten – who had finished in third place behind Wilkinson and Van Praag in heat five. Milne, like Bluey, had won his fourth race. This meant that the speedy Yank was just one point behind Wilkinson as the riders readied themselves for the fearful nineteenth heat. Although a victory for Milne and a second place for Wilkinson would have given them both 14 points, Bluey's 8 bonus points against Milne's 7 meant that second place for Wilkinson would be enough for him to claim the title. But it was not as straightforward as that. The great Jack Parker was in this heat, as was Milne's brother, Cordy. The younger Milne had won his second and third heats and Wilkinson could guarantee that, given the opportunity, Cordy would attempt to keep him back – holding Bluey in third place alongside a win for Jack Milne would translate to a run-off.

The tapes sprung up for what Wilkinson hoped would be the last race of the night, but his suspicions were fulfilled. The siblings bombed into first and second places, Jack in the lead. But Wilkinson, just in front of Parker, was not going to give up that easily. He fought his way past Cordy, but , for his brother's sake, he kept coming back at the dour Aussie, trying all he knew to move beyond the redhead's power. As it was, Wilkinson was able to split the Milne boys and take second place, snatching the title

65

West Ham's first World Champion, Bluey Wilkinson.

with 22 points, just one more than Jack Milne. Sportingly, the Milnes were the first to congratulate Bluey, who had ridden through a sea of pain throughout the entire contest. The extent of his injuries meant that he was to be the only champion to avoid the custom of being flung in the air by the other competitors. He had been in total agony, but his tenacity paid off. The whole arena got to its feet to acknowledge his intelligence and bravery.

Bedevilled by ill fortune in 1933 and 1936, Bluey Wilkinson had at last crowned his career and was Speedway World Champion. Bluey stars twinkled in a deep claret sky as the echo of 10,000 bike engines, revving in respect and affection reverberated around the dockland night. A translucent cloud of 'throttle mist' even seemed to turn the moon blue. Tower Bridge opened and set a silhouette like two crossed hammers over the city. Alongside the deep applauding hooters of great Antipodean ships, the whoops of tough little cockney tugs cheered the diminutive red-headed king of all the speedways. The river sang for Bluey.

'Lammy' Lamoreaux's winning race in heat fifteen was equal fastest time of the night, helping him to take third place. Van Praag finished fourth and Bill Kitchen, in joint fifth with Cordy Milne, got his best result to date. Three other West Ham riders made the final. Arthur Atkinson came joint tenth, Tommy Croombs achieved equal twelfth place, whilst the new Canadian signing, Jimmy Gibb, qualified as reserve but failed to get a ride and as such was not to become the second Canadian to appear in a World Championship final. Stylish England international Alec Statham finally saw his name on a World Final score sheet. Tommy Price made his debut in the World Final that year, as did American Benny Kaufman, who managed a commendable 7 points. Frank Varley and George Newton did not ride well, but Jack Ormston, the other reserve, scored a creditable 5 points from only two rides.

After his triumph, Wilkinson announced his retirement from riding. He took up a management position at Sheffield. 1938 was Bluey's – it was the climax of a brilliant career and he finished at the top.

1938 World Championship Final Score Chart
From left to right: Position, Rider, Country, Pts scored in each race, Ttl Pts, Bonus, Gd Ttl.

Pos	Rider	Country						Ttl Pts	Bonus	Gd Ttl
1	Bluey Wilkinson	Aus	3	3	3	3	2	14	8	22
2	Jack Milne	USA	3	3	2	3	3	14	7	21
3	Wilbur Lamoreaux	USA	3	1	3	3	3	13	7	20
4	Lionel Van Praag	Aus	3	2	2	1	3	11	7	18
5	Bill Kitchen	Eng	2	2	1	2	2	9	6	15
=	Cordy Milne	USA	1	3	3	0	1	8	7	15
7	Alec Statham	Eng	2	3	0	0	3	8	5	13
=	Eric Langton	Eng	1	2	2	3	0	8	5	13
9	Benny Kaufman	USA	2	1	0	2	2	7	5	12
10	Jack Parker	Eng	2	2	2	0	0	6	4	10
=	Arthur Atkinson	Eng	1	0	2	1	1	5	5	10
12	Tommy Price	Eng	1	0	1	2	0	4	4	8
=	Tommy Croombs	Eng	0	1	1	1	1	4	4	8
14	Geoff Pymar	Eng	0	0	1	0	1	2	5	7
=	George Newton	Eng	0	1	0	1	0	2	5	7
16	Frank Varley	Eng	0	0	0	ns	ns	0	4	4
	Jack Ormstom (res)	Eng				3	2	5	-	-
	Jimmy Gibb (res)	Can	Did not ride							

Heat	Riders	Time (secs)
1	Van Praag, Parker, Atkinson, Pymar	76.8
2	Lamoreaux, Stratham, C. Milne, Newton	75.0
3	J.Milne, Kaufman, Price, Croombs	77.4
4	Wilkinson, Kitchen, Langton, Varey	76.0
5	Wilkinson, Van Praag, Lamoreaux, Price,	76.2
6	C. Milne, Langton, Croombs, Pymar	77.8
7	Stratham , Parker, Kaufman,Varey	76.0
8	J.Milne, Kitchen, Newton, Atkinson	77.0
9	C. Milne, Van Praag, Kitchen, Kaufman,	77.2
10	Lamoreaux, J.Milne, Pymar, Varey	76.6
11	J.Milne, Langton, Van Praag, Stratham	75.8
12	Wilkinson, Atkinson, Croombs, Stratham,	78.0
13	Langton, Parker, Price, Newton	77.6
14	Wilkinson, Kaufman, Newton, Pymar	77.4
15	Lamoreaux , Kitchen, Croombs, Parker	76.0
16	Ormston, Price, Atkinson, C. Milne	77.6
17	Van Praag, Ormston, Croombs, Newton	78.2
18	Stratham, Kitchen, Pymar, Price,	76.8
19	J.Milne, Wilkinson, C. Milne, Parker	77.4
20	Lamoreaux, Kaufman, Atkinson, Langton	77.6

Bluey's Last Ride

Bluey Wilkinson did ride in 1939. At the behest of Johnnie Hoskins, the world champion turned out to support a charity meeting for a children's hospital. Viscountess Hinchinbroke (a regular visitor to Custom House) had helped arrange a Royal visit to the stadium for the event. Johnnie Hoskins had advertised the evening's contests, including the appearance of Wilkinson, before Bluey knew anything about the arrangements. Unfortunately, the Viscountess arranged for the Duchess of Kent to turn up on the Tuesday following Bank Holiday Monday, a traditional greyhound racing day at Custom House. There was no question that the dogs could be cancelled, so Hoskins was obliged to go back to his aristocratic contact and ask her to get the Duchess to shift her diary around.

By now Hoskins had made sure the stadium had built a special royal enclosure and box. The local council had already begun to bedeck the stadium with flowers and exotic trees. The Duchess managed to sort things out and a day was named for the first royal patronage of speedway. All that remained was for Hoskins to organise the appearance of the retired world champion. The first two phone calls gave no more information than 'Bluey's not in'. The next half-a-dozen calls were unanswered. At this point, Hoskins resorted to pleading in person and, after some persuasion, Wilkinson agreed to ride in a special Match Race series against Arthur Atkinson, who had taken over as West Ham's number one. Although he had not ridden for some months, Bluey beat Atkinson 2-0. The match complete, the Duchess, between being advised by members of the crowd to 'old on to yer 'at' in the presence of Johnnie, asked Hoskins if they were not to see more of the champion, but Wilkinson was never to ride again. Bluey was killed in a road accident in Australia in 1940.

Without Wilkinson, and with Stevenson's loss of power, West Ham fell down the League like a lead balloon.

Money For Speed

In 1938, with the average working wage at under £7 a week, a Birmingham promoter, Arthur Westwood, published the earnings of several of his Second Division team. Keith Harvey, a South African in the Brummie side, was said to earn £6 16s 2d a week on average. Skipper Tiger Hart was averaging just over £20 a week and even reserve Ted English made nearly £5 a week. Riders were paid 1½ d a mile for travelling and overnight expenses of 10s for hotel accommodation if the away trip was over 100 miles.

What about the speedway fans? Well, they were paying between 1s 3d and 5s admission at most First Division circuits. In the Second Division, prices were lower at between 6d and 2s. A Rudge with a JAP engine was available for the princely sum of about £49 10s.

6

WAR ENGINES

The Fence

The fence is for the protection of both public and riders. It serves, of course, to stop riders charging into the midst of spectators when losing control, and also serves as a guide to the riders during their races. There are two main types of fence – the wire mesh type, which is used mainly in grey-hound stadiums because they do not obstruct the view to the public for greyhound racing, and the solid fence which is used, for example, at football stadiums where it is unnecessary to see through the fence for any racing. Both these types of fence have advantages and disadvantages so far as the riders are concerned. The wire mesh fence has the advantage of being comparatively 'soft' to hit in the event of an accident; obviously the wire can stretch and give on impact. On the other hand, because of its very nature there is the possibility that a rider can become entangled in the fence if he rides too close to it and it is for this reason that a 'ride off' board is fitted to the bottom of the wire fence so that a rider's foot rest does not become entangled if he rides too close. The solid type of fence which can be composed of either wood or steel, is popular with the riders in some instances because it is easy to see. Riders are able to use it as a guide and in addition, on some tracks, like Exeter for example, which is steeply banked, they have even been known to use the fence in a close race to gain advantage by allowing their rear wheels to touch the fence and almost 'bounce' off down the banking at even greater speed! Of course the main complaint about the solid type of fence is that on impact it has no 'give' at all and a rider can sustain sometimes more serious injury if this happens than if the fence were of wire mesh.

Silver, L. 'Anatomy of a Speedway' in The Speedway Annual compiled by Silver, L. and Douglas, P. (London, Pelham Books, 1969)

West Ham were in fourth place in the League when war broke out in September 1939. Atkinson was now the side's 'main man', holding the fourth-highest score in the League. Croombs was his back-up and Jimmy Gibb was breaking into the third heat-leader position, usurping his fellow Canadian Eric 'Ricky' Chitty.

It was at about this time that a rider called Godfrey Rabie, a South African, came to West Ham. He was to become known as 'Scarface' during his brief stay. He made a few second-half rides and, in the process, succeeded in tearing down fencing, breaking both ankles and his nose, fracturing his jaw and picking up numerous minor injuries.

He returned to South Africa to regain fitness and was to fight with the 1st South African Brigade, part of Montgomery's Eighth Army, against Rommel's Afrika Korps. At Alamein, he was reputed to have single-handedly charged and destroyed a Nazi machine-gun emplacement on a motorbike, tommy-gun blazing between the handle bars. Evidently his 'adventurous' riding at Custom House had stood him in good stead.

The Second World War was to produce many stories relating to the strength and bravery of speedway riders. One of the most astounding of these tells of how Lionel Van Praag, who was a pilot during hostilities, was shot down off of the Australian Bite. The former World Champion, towing a wounded comrade, swam in the ocean for over twenty-four hours before being pulled out of the sea by a friendly vessel.

Arthur Atkinson was in the finest form of his career during 1939. He was selected for the Test series, turning out for England four times; in the first Test, he clocked up an 18-point maximum and, in the third match, he was his country's highest scorer, making a dozen points. He was to make double figures in the other two Tests, averaging 12.75 for the series – just short of top scorer Bill Kitchen. Kitchen had an extraordinarily rapid rise to fame. Within four months of his first ride for Belle Vue, he was in the English team. He served an 'apprenticeship' in sand and grass events and also competed in the Tourist Trophy road races in South America. Coming from Galgate, near Lancaster, he naturally joined Belle Vue and was one of the leading scorers at the Manchester club from 1933 onwards. Bill, who owned a motorcar business, rode with a typical Northern upright style, but always seemed to be held back by his relative lack of speed out of the gate.

In the World Championship, Atkinson was amongst the leading qualifiers, holding 6 bonus points for Wembley – just 2 less than 'Cowboy' Cordy Milne and 1 short of the estimable Kitchen, Lamoreaux and Langton. Eric Chitty was another Hammer who had fought his way to a place within the elite, carrying 5 points with him into the final. Although Milne was a clear favourite, there were many who reckoned that Atkinson's form during the year could take him to the title. There was, however, to be no final event in 1939.

The League was brought to a premature end when hostilities commenced, although speedway was to continue at Custom House. Johnnie Hoskins, not to be beaten even by Hitler's Fascist hordes, ran four wartime meetings in 1940, the first of which saw the Hammers defeat a combined New Cross and Wembley side 47-37 on 22 March. In April, Hoskins got the track ceremoniously reopened by the then Mayor of West Ham, Alderman Ted Wooder, 'defying the threat of tyranny'. The last of the four events that year saw Bill Longley triumph in the London Cup Trophy. Further wartime meetings were staged in 1941 and 1942.

Despite such defiance, as the shadow of the Blitz spread over the London docklands, an uneasy hush shrouded the terraces of West Ham Stadium and other tracks across Britain. Fully organised speedway was a costly and, in terms of oil and petrol, a somewhat profligate activity in a wartime economy. The Custom House arena did its war service, however, briefly being used as a transit site for prisoners of war waiting to be shipped on to camps throughout Britain. Given the threat to prisoners from the local population as they began to be tortured by bombing, this idea was soon scrapped.

There were occasional events in the London area throughout the war and fairly regular meetings at Belle Vue. The Manchester track even organised a British Individual Championship from 1940 to 1945. The winner of the first three tournaments was West Ham's Eric Chitty, who probably reached his peak during the war years. However, as the East End readied itself for battle, the bikes at Custom House for the most part fell silent. The roaring engines that would dominate cockney attention for the next five years would be those of Nazi bombers.

Following the war, rider allocation was imposed to ensure a fair spread of the star performers around the tracks. For example, Norman and Jack Parker rode for different teams for the first time: Jack for Belle Vue, Norman for Wimbledon. Norman proved to be a fine tactician and a great captain. He was an outstanding team rider, almost without equal. Under Norman's leadership, Wimbledon would win the National Trophy twice. He challenged his brother, Jack, for the Golden Helmet Match Race title, but, like so many challengers, was not successful. Norman was capped for his country on many occasions, and also captained England against the Australians a number of times.

The Boom Years

In common with other sports, speedway went through a boom period after the Second World War. However, conventional wisdom around the dirt holds the opinion that 'speedway was very popular after the war, but before the war it was another world'.

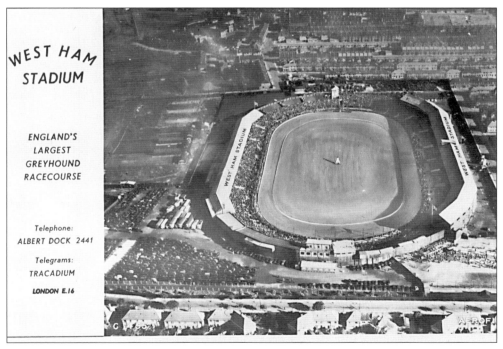

West Ham Stadium – home of the Hammers.

Indeed, it may be true to say that, by 1946, speedway had seen its golden years and that the late 1940s and early 1950s were something of a false dawn. Entertainment tax and television were just around the corner.

For all this, as early as 1946 the speedway was running smoothly again and flourished in Australia, New Zealand and in Britain. In the United Kingdom, it rivalled football as the most popular spectator sport. With crowd restrictions in force at the time, many meetings were held before capacity audiences. West Ham were drawing 60,000 fans to some matches, whilst an attendance of 40,000 was a disappointment. By 1947, there were three leagues and, as the 1940s became the 1950s, there were forty tracks operating. In the United States though it was a different story. Within a few years of the end of the Second World War, the influence of American riders was almost non-existent.

The post-war years started at Custom House on Good Friday, 19 April 1946. A huge crowd of 57,000 spectators witnessed the Hammers go down to 41-42 to Wembley in a challenge match. West Ham subsequently rejoined the National League.

Training and managerial changes at Custom House came with the peace. Throughout 1946, West Ham rented Hoddesdon Stadium (Rye House) every Wednesday, in order to give their riders extra practice, whilst team control was taken over by pre-war star, Arthur Atkinson, and the former New Cross rider, Stan Greatrex – who had started speedway having been inspired by Tom Farndon. Stan had begun his track career in 1931 at the Brandon Riders' School near his native town of Coventry, where he had

Left: *Malcolm Craven.* Right: *Buck Whitby.*

Youth and experience – Kid Curtis and Bob Harrison.

been employed in the car industry. Two years later, as one of the Coventry team, he broke all the local track records and held on to them for number of years. He was transferred to New Cross in 1934, making a good start and going on to be elected to skipper the side. Stan got his first Test outing in 1936. He was later to start a car business near the Coventry track.

Atkinson and Greatrex made a number of changes to the West Ham side. Frank Lawrence went to New Cross with Jack Cooley travelling the other way. Dick Geary moved to Sheffield and 'Crusty' Pye went to Middlesborough. There was also some enforced change. Colin Watson was seriously injured at Bradford on 13 July in a second-half scratch race. He crashed, hitting a lighting standard by the safety fence in the process. His machine dragged him, head down, for about sixty feet. Watson was taken to hospital where he was diagnosed as having punctured his lung and fractured his skull. Colin was unconscious and on the critical list for weeks. A calendar month later, during the qualifying round for the British Riders' Championship at Custom House, an announcement was made to the 60,000 crowd that Watson had taken a cup of tea and eaten a slice of bread and butter. The Beefeaters at the Tower could hear the roar of relief and support. Babies, sleeping in their cots in Barking, stirred at the rumble of care. Men, going on the nightshift at the Dagenham Ford plant, in recognition turned their eyes to the East and smiled. But Watson would never ride again. A benefit was arranged as the season grew old and over £2,000 was raised: the 60,000 gate was about fifteen per cent higher than the average attendance at West Ham Speedway at that time,

Benny King, who was sadly to take his own life.

although the last match of the season attracted a crowd in the region of 80,000. This was to be the largest post-war crowd at West Ham Stadium.

Eric Chitty was the grade one rider and skipper of the side, scoring 205 points in the National League. Only the great Jack Parker did better with 217. Malcolm Craven was vice-captain and the second heat-leader, whilst veteran Bob Harrison was the third-highest points taker. Harrison was among the first of the Manchester riders; after a spell with the White City (Manchester), he had joined Belle Vue in 1929 and was a steady scorer for them. Harrison was overshadowed by his partner, the great Eric Langton, but he won his share of races. He was equal second highest English scorer in his first Test match in 1930, but was not selected again until 1933. Harrison's next outing for his country didn't come until 1936. He often wintered in South America, and, in 1930, won the Argentine Tourist Trophy road race. However, after the Second World War the years were telling on Bob and he did not reach heat-leader standard whilst he was with the Hammers. Other riders turning out for West Ham that season included Benny King, Bert Rogers, George Gower, Wally Green, 'Buck' Whitby and Ron Howes – who had started out at Wimbledon as a mechanic and later worked with Vic Huxley before taking up riding. One of his most treasured possessions was a set of leathers that once were worn by the great 'Hux'. Ron was to leave the Hammers when Rayleigh Weir Stadium opened. He was made captain of that side and became very popular with the Essex fans.

West Ham, after Watson's injury, had no third heat-leader and this was instrumental in the team finding itself at the foot the table at the end of the season and their elimination, at the first round stage, from both the National Trophy and the London Cup. The side faired no better in ACU Cup table. With a mere 2 points, they finished at the very bottom.

In a desperate search for justice and/or relief, Atkinson and Greatrex protested. They insisted that a rider should be transferred from the overly strong Belle Vue side, as West Ham had been unforeseeably weakened by the loss and injury of key riders. After the Control Board management committee agreed to the West Ham recommendations, the full board overturned their decision, preferring a plan for a modified reallocation of riders in 1947.

The British Riders' Championship

With many riders still in the armed forces, and because many foreign riders had returned home during the war, an alternative tournament to the World Championship was run from 1947 to 1948. The British Riders' Championship was sponsored by the *Sunday Dispatch*. The majority of riders were British, and qualification was via six rounds. The hapless Hammers got some cheer from this contest, with Malcolm Craven and Eric Chitty making the final at Wembley. Craven reeled in 10 points and came equal fifth, just a single point ahead of Chitty. The Canadian came seventh. In the world

West Ham, 1946. From left to right: Benny King, Bob Harrison, Buck Whitby, Cyril Anderson, Malcolm Craven, Ron Howse, Jack Cooley and Eric Chitty on the bike.

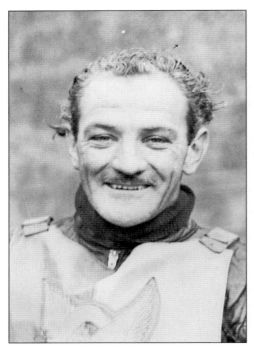

Left: *Vic Duggan – still smiling.* Right: *Jack Cooley, King of Crash No. 2, and West Ham mechanic Alec Mosely, with ubiquitous cigarette.*

rankings for 1946, the order was reversed: Chitty got tenth place, finishing ahead of Craven in twelfth. The British Riders' Championship was won by Tommy Price. He had caused some consternation by fitting a new rear wheel on his bike for each heat, providing optimum drive for each race. However, this was the start of a general slowing down in speedway, although the reasons for this are not altogether clear. Many years were to pass before track record times started to be broken again.

Turners, Tuners And Designers

In 1947, Wal Philips took charge of the Harringay workshops, having completed his racing days some years before. Their machines were the envy of many tracks, and it was Wal who was responsible for the tremendous speed of Vic Duggan's machines that were almost unbeaten that year. Philips played a large part in the design of the frame used by Vic at the time. His innovations, like the JAP engine of 1930, were revolutionary and he had a huge impact on the frame-building techniques of the time. The main difference was in the headlock where the forks joined the mainframe or 'diamond'. The older models were fitted with a ball-bearing joint, which was rather heavy and cumbersome. They were also fitted with a damper that could be turned to make the steering stiffer or looser. Duggan's frame was far simpler; a brass bush joined the headlock only. It looked more frail, but it was every bit as strong and much lighter. It was also far easier to handle. The frame was made lighter all round and it became known as the 'Aussie' frame because most of the Australian riders quickly started using it, with enormous success.

Alex Moseley, who was a contemporary of Philips, began his career as a sidecar racer and tuner at the famous Brooklands road-racing track. A master toolmaker by trade, he was the first man to tune and ride a sidecar machine at over 100 mph at that track – something of a feat in those days. When speedway started, Moseley linked up with the Wembley track, then under the direction of the Johnnie Hoskins. Moseley tuned for many great riders, including Sprouts Elder. When Hoskins moved from Wembley to West Ham in the early 1930s, Moseley went with him, and it was at West Ham that he became famous as one of the finest tuners and frame-builders in the business.

Aub Lawson – West Ham Messiah

During 1947, West Ham continued to rely on Chitty and Craven for the bulk of the team's points. The backward-looking attitude was reinforced by the reappearance of a pre-war star, Tommy Croombs, who came out of retirement to help his struggling Alma Mater. Croombs was not the rider he had once been, but his technical ability remained exemplary. The old gunslinger was still a white-line expert and he accumulated 124 points in 23 matches, becoming the third heat-leader in the process. However, the side was only separated from bottom club Harringay by a point at the end of the season.

Left: *Aub Lawson with his famous red scarf.* Right: *Malcolm Craven.*

Tommy Croombs and Malcolm Craven.

Australian Test Team, 1948. From left to right: Jack Biggs, Cliff Watson, Ray Duggan, Arthur Simcock (team manager), Vic Duggan, Bill Longley, Aub Lawson, Frank Dolan and Max Grossgreutz on machine.

Left: *The young Reg Fearman.* Right: *Bob Harrison.*

Aub Lawson receiving the Golden Helmet Match Race Championship from Sunday Pictorial's *Don Clarke and George Casey. Arthur Atkinson looks on (left).*

Eric Chitty was to have his best performance ever in the Riders' Championship in 1947. His 10 points gave him fourth place. In the world rankings, he stayed in the number ten spot, with Malcolm Craven moving into eleventh place.

As the 1948 season approached, West Ham put a great deal of faith into two developments: a new tarmac starting area (laid in May 1947) and an Australian import, Aub Lawson. The young Aussie wasted no time in impressing the Hammers' fans with his dynamic style and point-winning ability. His streaming chequered scarf quickly became almost as synonymous with victory as the flag that so often confirmed that he was first over the line. Lawson, a wartime dispatch rider, faced West Ham's opponents with a pitiless resolve that helped to drag the Hammers from their lowly status of the previous season to third place in the League. Lawson helped West Ham replicate the almost unconquerable form which they had shown on the 'Fortress Custom House' 440-yard circuit, away from the home citadel. In the nine away League matches he was involved in, Lawson scored at an average of 10.1. He rode in the five away cup matches and achieved an incredible average of 11.8. Even the great Australia and Harringay rider, Vic Duggan, could not match that in terms of away form. Such performances enabled flying Aub to qualify as a reserve for the Riders' Championship.

West Ham in the later 1940s. From left to right: Arthur Atkinson, Howdy Byford, Malcolm Craven, Bob Harrison, Tommy Croombs, Kid Curtis, Aub Lawson, Cliff Watson and Stan Greatrex. Eric Chitty is on the bike.

With Lawson alongside Chitty and Craven, it meant that West Ham now had a heat-leader trio of real power, but this was not replicated throughout the side and thus prevented them from winning the League. Another new signing, Cliff Watson, did well but, although Croombs could still offer elegance, this did not always pay off in points. Howdy Byford, in his first full year at Custom House, gave glimpses of form, but could not be relied on for a constant stream of results. During the Second World War, he had been one of those forced into slave labour on the Burmese railways by the Japanese. The reserves were Kid Curtis and Bob Harrison. In exasperation, West Ham attempted to sign up fifteen-year-old Reg Fearman, but were instructed by the Control Board that the minimum age for a team member was sixteen.

In the Riders' Championship, Malcolm Craven gained 6 points, which was enough to put him in equal ninth position. Eric Chitty, scoring just 5, came joint eleventh. This was his worst result in the competition to date. Even handicapped by his late start to the season, Lawson was ranked fourth in the world charts. Chitty was once again tenth, but Craven had dropped out of the top fifteen.

Also in 1948, Atkinson and Greatrex brought another innovation into the West Ham training set-up. A 300-yard practice circuit was built in the spacious car park of Custom House Stadium. It was designed to address the side's poor away form, acclimatising riders to the smaller circuits that existed at other clubs. The track was also used as a kind of academy, and a large numbers of youngsters could often be seen flying around the circuit. In May 1948, Reg Fearman received coaching on this circuit from Cliff Watson and Aub Lawson.

The latter part of the 1940s saw the formation of new, lower division teams. This opened the door to many young riders. For example, Bristol immediately absorbed four local grass-track riders: Johnny and Billy Hole, Dick Bradley and Roger Wise. It was not unusual for these smaller sides to act as nursery or training clubs for the bigger operations. Dagenham, who were known as the Daggers, played this role for West Ham. They rode at Poole Lane in the late 1940s (the stadium was demolished in the 1950s to make way for the development of the Ford Motor Company).

By 1948, the entry list for the British Riders' Championship had become far more cosmopolitan, and on this basis the World Final was re-instated on 22 September 1949 at Wembley, in front of 93,000 fans. The 224 entrants were reduced to sixteen finalists via qualifying rounds. English rider Norman Parker was third highest qualifier, but Tommy Price won the final, beating Norman's brother, Jack, into second place.

7
THROUGH THE GAP ON A JAP

The Tractor Driver

Apart from the necessary ability to be able to drive a tractor, this important staff member must, like the rakers, know the most popular 'line' of the riders, for he must use his grader to re-cover and smooth out as much of the surface as possible between races. He must also take great care in his manoeuvres, for if he is careless, he may catch the safety fence with his grader and pull a large section down, creating havoc in the midst of a meeting. A good tractor driver can make the job of weekly track maintenance much easier, for by replacing the shale properly between races, he can avoid any damage being caused to the base material of the track, and it is this kind of damage that causes a track maintenance man the greatest headaches. The tractor is fitted with a blade used in track preparation. An angled blade is lowered on to the ground and set square. It works hydraulically and screw fittings can angle it in all directions. As the tractor moves forward the blade shifts the loose shale to one side, leaving a continuous heap of shale all around the track. The blade is then reset at right angles to the tractor and the shale is moved to its required position. Then the grader is fitted instead of the blade and this levels it to make it smooth to race on.
Silver, L. 'The Vital Cogs' in *The Speedway Annual* compiled by Silver, L. and Douglas, P. (London, Pelham Books, 1969)

The JAP reigned over speedway unchallenged for over thirty years. In the late 1940s, most West Ham riders continued to favour the five-stud JAP engine. These machines were fuelled with Castrol R. Many lovers of speedway in the post Second World War period say they knew of no sweeter smell than Castrol burning out of a JAP. Frames made by the Excelsior Company were successful in the years leading up to the Second World War, with riders like Lionel Van Praag favouring them. They were used again after the hostilities, up until about 1947, when the advent of the lighter, modern frames started to be pioneered by Australia and Harringay rider Vic Duggan.

West Ham encouraged the experimental Vincent bike in 1948; Tommy Croombs rode the machine regularly that season. The bike was reliable and could be coaxed to produce around 40hp. It also weighed less than the JAP at 54lb (including carb and magneto).

In the late 1940s, Philip Vincent combined with Australian designer and engineer Phil Irving, seeking to develop a 500cc engine capable of matching the dominant speedway JAP. One cylinder head and barrel from a Rapide V-twin road bike motor was used, bolted to a specifically ordered magnesium alloy crankcase. West Ham were impressed with the machine and sought the distribution rights, but Vincent protested and cancelled the project. As such, just twenty-five of the lightweight crankcases were made, but only thirteen speedway engines were completed.

As the 1950s began, the post-war speedway boom years came to a peak. England, in addition to 1949 World Champion Tommy Price, boasted such riders as Jack Parker, Bill Kitchen and Split Waterman; the future looked bright, but there were signs of danger. Crowds were falling away after the immediate post-war upsurge, and interest in Australia, for more than twenty years a pipeline of fresh talent to the British Leagues, was on the decline, even though an Australian, Jack Young, won the world title in 1951 and 1952.

When the Stanley Park stadium in Liverpool re-opened in 1949, Brian Craven (elder brother of Peter) started the speedway 'bug' in the family when he progressed from cycle speedway to the 'real thing'. West Ham's Aub Lawson carried his fine form to Australia over the winter. He was ranked number one in his native land, pushing aside the likes of Vic Duggan. On his return to Custom House for the 1949 term, Lawson was often fighting single-handedly, especially on trips away from the East End, Tommy Croombs having retired once and for all and Eric Chitty picking up an injury after only six matches that was to keep him out for the rest of West Ham's campaign. Chitty had wintered in Australia from 1947, but never really excelled there and was noted more for his bitter complaints about his rates of pay than his performances on the track. He crashed and broke his leg during his final appearance Down Under, in the Australian Four-lap Championship at the Brisbane Exhibition Ground on 16 February 1949. It is likely that this was part of the problem that caused his absence from the West Ham side when he returned to Custom House.

To make matters worse, Malcolm Craven was not the power of former times. At this point, he was riding the Vincent Vampire. This beautifully copper-plated machine was introduced onto the speedway tracks of Britain in 1948 – it has been suggested that a chromium shortage after the Second World War necessitated the copper frame. However, Cliff Watson was developing. He became third heat-leader following a gradual improvement in his riding. At the start of the season, he was paired with Lawson. Prior to their parting in July, they had scored an impressive 159 points from a maximum 180. Within this, the pair recorded twenty-two 5-1 scores, seven 4-2s and seven 3-3s. As a pair, they won every race they entered.

Howdy Byford's form continued to be erratic, so Wally Green was brought back from Hastings, where he had been on loan. The two reserves were Kid Curtis and Frank Bettis. Reg Fearman came into the side, making seven appearances and scoring 4 points.

Another strengthening measure involved bringing George Wilks in on loan from Wembley as a temporary replacement for Chitty. Wilks was among the most promising

Cliff Watson explains a part of the JAP engine to fifteen-year-old Reg Fearman.

The skipper of Harringay, Vic Duggan.

Brother Hammers – Reg Fearman and Frank Bettis.

'Whats the score?' Eric Chitty and Reg Fearman approach the track from the pits in front of the West Ham score board (rakers in the foreground).

The caricature is titled "THE HAMMERS of '49" and dated 26·4·1949. Labels within the image read: SOME IMPRESSIONS AT WEST HAM SPEEDWAY; CLIFF WATSON (WOT NO WHISKERS?); GEORGE WILKS ON LOAN FROM WEMBLEY; HOWDY BYFORD; KID CURTIS; STAN GREAT AND ARTH ATKINS; ING SKIPPER B LAWSON; EST HAM'S SONS F AUSTRALIA; E ING MER LCOLM AVEN; REG FEARMAN OF PLAISTOW RECEIVES, ON HIS SIXTEENTH BIRTHDAY HIS RIDERS CONTRACT FROM THE INJURED HAMMERS SKIPPER – ERIC CHITTY; OLD TIMER COLIN WATSON; WALLY GREEN; BENNY KING; FRANK BETTIS; THE HAMMERS JUNIORS FOR WHOM OPPORTUNITY KNOCKS; THE POPULAR MANAGERS.

The Hammers of 1949.

of the younger speedway riders in the early days of the sport. Always a keen motorcyclist, he became involved in competition in 1927. He learnt the basis of technique on the Barnet grass-track, not far from where he was born in Watford, Hertfordshire. He gained his first chance on first-class tracks when he joined Harringay. Wilks made rapid progress after joining Hackney Wick in 1936, and developed into a sound team-rider. He helped Hackney to win the London Cup and rode for London against Australia. He was a motor mechanic by trade. Entering the veteran stage, he rode well enough for West Ham, achieving an average of 6.25.

West Ham did enough at Custom House to make sure of fourth place in the League at the end of the season. They were also able to get themselves to the finals of the National Trophy and the London Cup, but their form away from home continued to be abysmal. In the away leg of the National Trophy final, they were ripped to pieces 78-30, killing their chances of making up the deficit at Custom House. With 14 points, Lawson was the only rider able to hold his head up. The team's morale plummeted and could not be raised by the home leg. They embarrassed themselves and the supporters by going down 62-46 at Custom House, again Lawson alone battled bravely, scoring 15.

Having qualified for the final of the World Championship, which was reinstated in 1949, Lawson lost concentration on the night. He managed just 8 points, going home in equal seventh position. Cliff Watson was another qualifying Hammer but, with just a single point, he ended up fifteenth. Thomas Arthur Price became the first Englishman to win the crown. Tommy Price was born in Lancashire at Burscough Bridge in 1907. He started his speedway career with Preston soon after the sport reached England. He retired after riding for several Northern tracks, but came back in 1934 to assist Birmingham when that team was revived. Tommy went back to Lancashire to skipper the Liverpool side in 1936. He was runner-up in that year's Provincial Riders' Championship, finishing only 2 points behind the winner, George Greenwood.

England gained only the second 1-2-3 in the World Championship in 1949. Louis Lawson of Belle Vue finished third, whilst Jack Parker was runner-up. Parker was one of the most likeable personalities in speedway at the time and was renowned for his sense of humour. He came to speedway through his work in a motorcycle manufacturer's experimental department. Jack led Coventry, and in 1929 was runner-up in the English Riders' Championship. In 1931, when skipper of Southampton, he won the British Open Championship from Vic Huxley in a series of epic races. Twelve months later, he had to relinquish the title owing to injury. He moved to Clapton in 1932, and in 1934 went on to Harringay. He rode in the first ever Test match and became an automatic choice for the English side.

When European speedway began to boom in the late 1940s, the structure of the World Championship had to be revised. In 1949, the bonus points system was dropped. Instead, a series of qualifying rounds and semi-finals decided the sixteen riders who would take part in the final. The points scored on final night determined the winner.

Lawson's form over the season was sufficient to rocket him up to second place in the world rankings. Aub finished just above the new champion, Tommy Price, and only Jack Parker, the World Championship runner-up, kept him from top spot.

West Ham at the start of the 1950s. From left to right, back row: Reg Fearman, Lloyd Goffe, Eric Chitty, Howdy Byford, Arthur Atkinson, Johnny Guilfoyle. Front row: Aub Lawson, Wally Green, Malcolm Craven, Kid Curtis.

West Ham, 1949. From left to right: Arthur Atkinson, Kid Curtis, Trevor Davis, Malcolm Craven, Lloyd Goffe, Wally Green, Howdy Byford, Reg Fearman, Aub Lawson, Ted Argall, Stan Greatrex and Eric Chitty on machine.

Tiger Stevenson tutors Reg Fearman with the aid of a 1928 Douglas loaned to Reg by Aub Lawson.

West Ham in the mid 1950s. From left to right: Howdy Byford, Cliff Watson, Kid Curtis, Frank Bettis, Wally Green, George Wilks and Aub Lawson on the bike.

West Ham v. Wimbledon, 1949. Howdy Byford and Kid Curtis of West Ham hold off Jimmy Gibb of Wimbledon.

As the first half of the twentieth century came to a close, Atkinson and Greatrex, in an attempt to promote speedway and look for potential new talent, allowed youngsters to take part in a one-lap races on push bikes on the Custom House track. Pushbike dirt-track racing, which had started on bombsites and streets, was becoming popular as an organised sport and speedway had begun to recruit the better performers into the motorised ranks. One winner of a race was a sixteen-year-old by the name of Grimstead. The lad was to grow up to become one of the East London's leading businessmen, dealing in bikes and motorcycles.

On 21 June 1949, West Ham were involved in a match with Bradford, which was broadcast live on television. The veteran Joe Abbot was riding. Joe, who was an extremely skilful rider, even at the age of forty-seven, learnt to broadside in Burnley, Lancashire, where he was born in 1902. Abbot was the mainstay of the Preston team between 1930 and 1931 before moving to Belle Vue in 1932. His steadiness and unselfishness made him an ideal team rider. He and Frank Charles did well together for the big Manchester club and also for England in Test matches. Abbott made up a famous Test partnership with Tom Farndon. However, Joe had suffered several serious injuries during his long career, some of which would have caused any less determined rider to retire. He had another crash that day in June when the crowd included dozens of ambulance men from Poplar Hospital, watching the meeting as part of a social event. It goes without saying that they got Joe to hospital immediately, forgoing the usual need for an emergency telephone call.

Australian team, Bradford, 1947. From left to right: Aub Lawson, Max Grosskreutz, Bill Longley, Johnnie Hoskins, Lionel van Praag, Frank Dolan, Ray Duggan, Vic Duggan, Doug McLaughlin.

Dashing Hammer, Cliff Watson.

As the new decade started at West Ham, there was a change in management. Alan D. Sanderson acquired the licence and brought Johnnie Hoskins back as promoter. Former rider Ken Brett was installed as team manager. Despite the changes, the Hammers continued their slow slide down the table. Eric Chitty came back, but he looked like a spent force. Malcolm Craven was still good, however, like Chitty, he had seen better days. Aub Lawson continued to be the Hammers' kingpin. He was abetted by Wally Green. Following a season acclimatising himself back into the team, Green became one of the club's best riders and, alongside Lawson, was the only other dependable performer on the Custom House riding staff. Cliff Watson's form plummeted and an exchange deal was arranged mid-season, which brought Lloyd Goffe to Custom House from Harringay. However, a curse seemed to be hanging over the East End. Byford was plagued by injury and illness and Reg Fearman was not able fulfil his obvious potential. Kid Curtis kept his role as the other reserve.

Having reached the last four, West Ham were eliminated from the London Cup. They had beaten Second Division Walthamstow in the first round. The Hammers went out of the National Trophy at a similar stage, beaten 121-94 by Bradford. On the bright side, Aub Lawson achieved the remarkable exploit of taking Jack Parker's Match Race title in August. Three years earlier, Vic Duggan had been the last rider to accomplish this feat.

91

West Ham, 1949. From left to right: Aub Lawson, Reg Fearman, Cliff Watson and Kid Curtis.

In the World Championship final, Aub finished in fourth place with 10 points. Wally Green supplied the shock of the evening by taking second place, a single point behind Freddie Williams – the first Welshman to win the speedway crown. It was Green's first appearance in a Wembley final and he was never seen again in such elite company. Dropping a place to third in the world rankings, Lawson was passed by a new wonder-kid from his homeland, Graham Warren. Wally Green's exploits in the World Championship took him to twelfth, one place behind another up-and-coming Australian, Jack Young, who rode for Edinburgh.

In the 1949/50 winter season, Ronnie Moore started using a JAP machine and his results improved dramatically. In 1949 he won his first major title, the South Island Championship. Norman Parker, then captain of the Wimbledon speedway team, was touring New Zealand and suggested to Ronnie's father, Les, that his son should try his luck in England, thinking that he had the talent to make the grade in British speedway. Parker signed the young Moore to ride for Wimbledon, and it was Norman who taught Ronnie the art of team riding. In February 1950, Ronnie sailed for England. He arrived in March, just in time for the start of the British season at Wimbledon Speedway – his first and last English club.

His first practice appearance was not auspicious and included taking a rather crude tumble on the Plough Lane shale. However, he had done enough to convince the Wimbledon promoter, Ronnie Greene, that he should be given a second-half ride in Wimbledon's first senior meeting of the season. At the tender age of seventeen, Moore made his debut.

Ronnie's first official ride on the Wimbledon track was a second-half, two-lap Match Race against Wimbledon junior George Butler. Ronnie won his first contest and his reward was to be included in the following week's second-half meeting, where he finished in last place in his first ride, but won well in his second. Ronnie was given a reserve place in a ten-man Wimbledon team that took on the famous Wembley Lions the following week in a challenge match. He won his side just 2 points, but kept his place in the line-up for the following contest, a Spring Cup meeting against Bristol. He scored a reserve's maximum from his two rides. By the start of May, Moore was in the team proper and, with his father, Les, had won a best pairs trophy in Ireland.

Ronnie's scoring continued to improve as the season went on, earning him his first international cap when he was picked as reserve for the Kangaroos in the England *v.* Australia Test match held at Wimbledon in July. Protests were made because he was, in fact, a New Zealander, but he had actually been born in Tasmania. He became the youngest rider ever to represent Australia.

Wimbledon promoter Ronnie Green, keen to give his new star extra rides, appointed him captain of the Shelbourne Tigers in Dublin, his father's old track. Moore soon became as popular in Ireland as he was in England. Ronnie won the Irish Open Championship in Dublin from a quality field of First Division riders.

The highlight of Ronnie's season, however, was still to come as he slammed in a 15-point maximum to win the Wimbledon World Championship qualifying round, beating among others the reigning World Champion, Tommy Price, his own skipper, Norman Parker, and the Harringay star, Split Waterman. This score, when added to the 7 points scored at Bradford and 12 at Wembley, was enough to see Ronnie through to

Left: *Aub Lawson going round the bend.* Right: *Fred 'Kid' Curtis.*

his first World Final – to become the youngest ever World Finalist at only seventeen years of age, a record never to be equalled. He scored 7 points.

Peter Craven got his first ride the same year at his hometown track in Liverpool, borrowing his brother Brian's machine. It was Peter's sixteenth birthday. He did a few laps and then promptly hit the safety fence, sustaining concussion. This damped his ardour for a few months, and he did not ride again until the winter, when he joined other young riders at the Ainsdale Sands practice track.

1951 saw the continued improvement of Aub Lawson. Yet again his average was West Ham's best, producing a League high of 10.12. He rode to victory in the London Riders' Championship and took the Wimbledon track's Laurels event in immaculate style. Lawson began the season by beating off World Champion Freddie William's assault on his Match Race title, but he was not successful when Jack Parker came to call. Perhaps placing some hope in the Lawson genes, West Ham gave Aub's half-brother, Don, a few rides. Whilst he didn't do too badly, it was clear that if speedway genius is hereditary, it came from a line of which Aub was a part and Don was not.

Malcolm Craven started to look more like his former self with an improvement in form and Eric Chitty, whilst getting nowhere near his best, improved on his 1950 performance. Wally Green could not fulfil the potential he had shown in the previous year's World Championship, with an average of 7.2. Byford continued to disappoint. Reg Fearman began to display touches of the promise he had shown as a

West Ham, 1952. From left to right, back row: Colin Clark, Pat Clark, Johnnie Hoskins, Cliff Watson, Howdy Byford. Front row: Kid Curtis, Wally Green, Jack Young, Malcolm Craven.

Bill Matthews, Cliff Watson and Vic Duggan in the West Ham pits.

boy, but National Service claimed him mid-season, probably robbing West Ham's future of a strong and able rider. Kid Curtis maintained his seemingly perennial role of reserve.

Looking to push his side on, Arthur Atkinson re-entered track tussling. However, the years had taken a lot away from the old master and, by the end of the season, his comeback could not be said to have been altogether successful. He was soon to go on to run the side at Rayleigh, together with his wife 'Tippy'. He would take Ron Howes and Charlie Mugford with him. At that time, there was a small glass building near the start line at Rayleigh, which was just about able to accommodate a couple of people. On race nights potted flowers surrounded it, to the extent that it appeared to be a bank of blooms. During a sidecar meeting, racing clockwise, as was the custom in such events, a machine lost control, evicted its passenger and crashed at high speed into the seeming bank. The building was effectively demolished as the whole vehicle took to the air like a plane at take-off. Its 'flight path' sent it ripping through a tangle of electricity cables, the consequence of which was that the whole stadium was blacked-out. Tippy, who had been inside the building with Jack Agambar, the starting-line marshal, had instinctively thrown herself to the ground and effectively saved herself, but Jack staggered from the wreckage covered in blood. Having taken a shower of glass, wood and metal straight in the face, he had sustained a mass of injuries. It took him many months to recover.

Meanwhile at West Ham, Malcolm Craven's improved form helped the team better their League performance of the previous term, gaining a creditable fourth place, although the Hammers were not title contenders at any stage. Managing to get to the second round of the National Trophy and the semi-final of London Cup, 1951 turned out to be respectable year rather than a successful one for West Ham. This was confirmed by Lawson's World Championship form. He finished equal eighth with Bob Leverenz, both scoring 7 points. Lawson would eventually replace Leverenz at Norwich. Jack Young won the world title in front of a crowd of 93,000. Almost immediately, Belle Vue and New Cross were offering to take Jack out of the Second Division and into the top flight of League speedway.

The 1951 World Championship was Ronnie Moore's second. He finished fourth with 11 points. He also topped the Wimbledon points averages for the first time, earned further Australian Test caps, helped Wimbledon to win the National Trophy and won a second Irish Championship.

The three fastest heats of the World Final were all won in a time of 70.6 seconds. This was only bettered in the 1975 event at Wembley when Ole Olsen (heat four) and Ivan Mauger (heat sixteen) both recorded 70.4 seconds. Whilst the circuit in the mid-1970s was in poor condition and the actual shape of the Wembley track always varied slightly – as it had to be cut under the football pitch – the machinery of the 1970s was certainly superior to that of 1951. From this it could be argued that the riders of the early 1950s were the best the world has ever seen.

Also in 1951, Peter Craven was given a try-out for Liverpool, but he hit the fence again after only one lap. In spite of this minor setback, he was included in the team as reserve for an away match against Leicester. His lack of inches and youthful looks had their disadvantages. On a number of occasions, track staff on Liverpool's away trips turned him away because they could not believe that one who looked so young could be a rider. During that season he made 8 league appearances for the Chads in Division Two, scoring 8 points.

Aub Lawson held on to third place in the world rankings. Jack Young was top man, holding off Split Waterman. At the end of the season, Lawson, as was his wont, wintered in Australia. He was victorious in the Australian Championship and in the Test series gained the distinction of being top scorer. Such was his success that he decided to resist the delights that Custom House might offer in 1952 and stay on Down Under. He would never again defend the dirt of Custom House or don the claret and blue. Aub was known as the 'Gentleman of the Speedways', and he was one of that rare band of sportspeople who could combine civility, politeness and humanity (towards fellow professionals, officials and supporters), with skill, bravery and exciting performances that never failed to entertain. He also never lost his temper. One ACU steward was so impressed by Lawson's conduct that he wrote to the Control Board manager, Major Fearnley: 'I would like to commend to the Board the manner in which Aub Lawson, captain of West Ham, carries out his duties, for his gentlemanly bearing and unfailing courtesy with help and advice, always available to the steward if required.'

Riders On The Storm

West Ham could not spend much time in mourning; they had to find a replacement. They chose Jack Young, the World Champion. In 1952, West Ham Speedway witnessed the tragic death of the young American rider, Ernie Roccio. The twenty-five-year-old died the day after crashing at Custom House on 22 July.

Death gives way to life. Bored with life as an office boy in an advertising agency in his native Christchurch, New Zealand, Barry Briggs followed his boyhood idol, Ronnie Moore, to England and Wimbledon at the start of that season. He was a raw, tall (for a speedway rider at 5ft 10in), gangling, awkward, inexperienced novice, whose 'head-down-and-at-them' attitude often outpaced his skill. The seventeen-year-old Briggs did everything wrong. Too much throttle at all the wrong times often sent him crashing to the Plough Lane track. He caused several terrible pile-ups and other riders wanted to ban him because he was too dangerous. But Wimbledon were plagued by injuries that season, so he got his chances, persevered and, by the end of the term, he had earned a regular place in the team.

It took a record fee of £3,500 to bring Jack Young to Custom House. No transfer fee surpassed this sum for two decades. Young took on Lawson's mantle as West Ham's lone wolf, the one true fighter in the West Ham pack. Malcolm Craven and Green lacked consistency; Byford and Curtis failed to develop and, although Cliff Watson was back from a sojourn with Harringay, he was not able to replicate the form that had made him a contender in World Championship final. However, Pat Clarke, who had come to West Ham at the start of the season, produced a creditable average of 4.7. Young's average for the year was 10.7. He was only bettered in the League by Ronnie Moore's gargantuan 11-point average. Wal Morton was back, but his 1.7 average failed to excite. 'Rugged' Reg Reeves, West Ham's 'Mad Dog' of the track, rode a few times, but even his ferocious attitude could do little to help the Hammers clock out of the League higher than fourth place. West Ham had effectively been in stasis. The strange mixture of brilliance and mediocrity had its predictable consequences in the cup competitions. In the National Trophy, the Custom House boys were unceremoniously booted out in the first round and, whilst they did slightly better in the London Cup, not being eliminated until the semi-final, this was hardly an impressive performance.

8

JACK YOUNG WEST HAM'S SECOND WORLD CHAMPION

The Track

Naturally the main piece of equipment is the track itself, and in modern day speedway this is usually composed of either red shale or granite dust. Both have similar qualities and are used in different stadiums purely on the basis of local availability. Most tracks are similar in shape, containing two straights and two bends, but their actual size and shape is usually dictated by the stadium in which they are built. There are very few stadiums which were built for the specific purpose of speedway racing. In fact in England there is only one, and that is Belle Vue, Manchester. The tracks therefore vary considerably in size and even in shape. The Sheffield track is almost circular, whilst the Newport track is very 'square'. When the track is originally made, the contractors have first to put down some form of hard base. This can be clinker or brick rubble or any similar form of material, and it is important that this base is level before putting on the top surface of shale or granite. The beauty of shale or granite is that whilst it is a sand-like substance to use in the first instance, it very quickly binds itself together and goes hard, setting rather as concrete does, excepting that when it is watered the very top layer breaks away again, to make the loose surface which the riders slide on.

Silver, L. 'Anatomy of a Speedway' in *The Speedway Annual* compiled by Silver, L. and Douglas, P. (London, Pelham Books, 1969)

Despite his side's unremarkable season, Jack Young was able to mark his quality in the World Championship. An innovation in the means of qualifying involved Continental riders being granted their own eliminating rounds. This was in recognition of their growing prowess. Early meetings were held in West Germany and Norway, with later Scandinavian rounds organised in Denmark, Sweden, Finland and again in Norway. This provided qualifiers for a Scandinavian Final in Oslo and a Continental Final in Munich. The best riders from these events went through to the European Grand Final at Falkoping in Sweden. Another departure from tradition was the involvement of five British riders – Reg Morgan, Bob Mark, Jim Gregory, Tony Lewis and Hammer Ken

*Jack Young, World Champion
Hammer, 1953.*

McKinlay – in the Scandinavian
and Continental contests. Only
Gregory progressed to the
British International qualifiers.

In Britain, the top twenty-four
from ninety-six riders in the first
national round made it to the
international section. Here they
were joined by the six best from
Falkoping and sixty-six men from
Division One and Two clubs. The
top sixty then entered the
Championship round on tracks
in Division One, where twenty of
the best riders from the top flight
entered the fray. Each competitor
had two qualifying meetings: the
top scorers were Bob Oakley on
28 and Jack Young, Split Waterman,
Ronnie Moore and Freddie
Williams, each with 27 points.

For the first time since the start of the Second World War, the contest for the final at
Wembley was in, every sense, an international one. South African Henry Long and
Sweden's Dan Forsberg were their respective nations' first representatives in the World
Finals. Basse Hveem was the first rider from Norway to make it to Wembley, although
he was not called upon to ride, having only made the reserve berth.

Jack Young, now a First Division rider, was better prepared for the big atmosphere of
Wembley and well fancied to retain his title. Added to this, one of his main rivals, Split
Waterman, came to the event with a cracked kneecap. However, top qualifier Bob
Oakley was a bit of a mystery and, as such, a dangerous foe. Both he and Williams had
the advantage of riding on their home league track. They knew the most effective
technique in terms of handling the starting gate. Derek Close, Ron How, Arthur Forrest,
Brian Crutcher, Forsberg and Long were all first-timers, as were the reserves, Hveem
and Trevor Redmond. Notable absentees were Jack and Norman Parker, Bill Kitchen,
Tommy Price and Aub Lawson.

Although the Final was not as thrilling as some that had gone before, technically it
represented speedway at its finest and was a meeting of the highest quality. The
manner in which Young seemed almost laid-back in defence of his title showed his
confidence as a Champion. Young's two deadly adversaries – and the men most likely
to relieve him of his title – were Freddie Williams and Split Waterman, the latter having

defied doctor's orders to compete. Although in great pain, he rode hard. The trio came together in the sixth heat. The stadium fell silent as the rivals lined up, straining at the tapes like latter-day horsemen of the apocalypse. With a magnificent thunderclap of horsepower, the bikes flew into action. As they burst through rev-induced fog, Jack saw the back of Waterman's bike and, beyond that, the tail of the Welsh Dragon disappearing into the distance. Young had missed the gate, but head down, the fighting Hammer willed himself to tug in Waterman. On the second lap, he bore down on and passed the Split personality. Now he was chasing the Deadly Druid. Coming up on Williams, Young attempted to take the initiative from the inside, but the Terrible Taff seemed to have psychic powers and was able to hold off the West Ham lightening dog. Young then threw his assault to the outside of Williams, but again, like the man of Harlech that he was, the Welshman would not yield. The crowd were ecstatic as Kangaroo Young went through his repertoire of tactics, but Welsh wizard Williams was a past master of track chess and foiled the Aussie Acrobat's every move.

The pair smashed into the last lap with every drop of pain, will and speed available to them. On the back straight, like twin banshees fleeing the worst flames of hell, locked together in the mad mesmerism of the race, Young and Williams plunged onward, leaving a cloud of dirt and smoke in their combined wake. At this point, Young abandoned suave intelligence and racing grace, taking on a more aggressive stance that put brute force to the fore. Ramming into the home straight, the pair were still screeching and bellowing as a single entity. Not a soul in the arena – man, woman or child – was in their seat. The winner would be the ultimate victor – the tsar of all the tracks. They cannoned over the line. Half the stadium celebrated a Williams win, the other yelped for Young; the applause was as much of a melee as the race. In the end, it was the width of a tyre that decided the destination of the title.

This race exemplified Young's solitary weakness and his ultimate strength. He was perfection in every facet of his riding, but he suffered from the curse of the starting line. He was doomed to cogitation before acceleration. There is no real explanation for this malaise, and Young never found a cure for the disease. Again and again, he was left at the gate and obliged to make his strike from the rear. His situation made for some electrifying encounters and epic clashes, but Young, throughout his career, struggled to overcome his initial inertia. He told Tommy Price, 'I wish I could trap', Price, with no thought at all, retorted: 'Well, Jack, thank Christ you can't or we might as well all pack it in.'

Jack Young won the World Championship for the second time in consecutive years. He was the first rider to achieve this. No one would win the title twice in succession for a further six years and it took eighteen years to better Young's World Championship feat. Williams and Oakley made the most of their 'home track' knowledge, finishing second and third respectively. Forrest, the 'Black Prince', also demonstrated that he had a good deal of potential with excellent rides in his last two races. Forsberg did Sweden proud, defeating Williams and Oakley in heat fourteen. At this point in the proceedings, both the British riders were still in with a chance of the title. If the Swede had avoided falling in the last heat, he may have forced Oakley into a third-place run-off. Brian Crutcher was the youngest rider in the event. The eighteen-year-old's determination defeated his nerves, snatching heat five on the last bend from Jeff Lloyd.

From left to right: Position, Rider, Country, Pts scored in each race, Ttl.

1	Jack Young	Aus	3	3	3	3	2	14
2	Fred Williams	Wales	3	2	3	2	3	13
3	Bob Oakley	Eng	3	3	2	1	3	12
4	Ronnie Moore	NZ	2	2	3	f	3	10
5	Arthur Payne	Aus	0	1	2	3	3	9
=	Dan Forsberg	Swe	2	3	1	3	f/r	9
=	Dick Bradley	Eng	3	2	3	1	0	9
8	Jeff Lloyd	Eng	2	2	0	2	1	7
=	Arthur Forrest	Eng	1	1	0	3	2	7
=	Henry Long	S Afr	1	0	2	2	2	7
11	Brian Crutcher	Eng	1	3	1	0	1	6
=	Split Waterman	Eng	2	1	0	1	2	6
13	Graham Warren	Aus	0	1	1	2	1	5
14	Derek Close	Eng	1	0	2	0	1	4
15	Cyril Roger	Eng	0	exe	1	1	0	2
16	Ron How	Eng	0	ef	0	0	0	0
=	Trevor Redmond (res)	NZ	Did not ride					
=	Basse Hveem (res)	Nor	Did not ride					

The Blond Bombshell – Graham Warren of Australia. West Ham refused to sign him towards the end of the 1940s, but he eventually joined Birmingham to become an overnight sensation.

Heat	Riders	Time (secs)
1	Williams, Moore, Close, Payne	69.6
2	Oakley, Lloyd, Forrest, How	70.4
3	Young, Forsberg, Long, Warren	70.4
4	Bradley, Waterman, Crutcher, Roger	71.2
5	Crutcher, Lloyd, Warren, Close	71.8
6	Young, Williams, Waterman, How (ef)	70.6
7	Forsberg, Moore, Forrest, Roger (exe)	70.2
8	Oakley, Bradley, Payne, Long	70.6
9	Bradley, Close, Forsberg, How	71.4
10	Williams, Long, Roger, Lloyd	71.0
11	Moore, Oakley, Warren, Waterman	70.6
12	Young, Payne, Crutcher, Forrest	71.4
13	Forrest, Long, Waterman, Close	71.2
14	Forsberg, Williams, Oakley, Crutcher	71.6
15	Young, Lloyd, Bradley, Moore (f)	72.4
16	Payne, Warren, Roger, How	72.2
17	Oakley, Young, Close, Roger	72.0
18	Williams, Forrest, Warren, Bradley	72.4
19	Moore, Long, Crutcher, How	72.4
20	Payne, Waterman, Lloyd, Forsberg (f/re)	72.2

In 1952, Young showed his all-round brilliance as a team member and as a champion. But he also demonstrated his ability as a Match Racer, taking the Match Race title from Ronnie Moore, who, for the second year running, finished fourth in the World Championships with 10 points. That year, Moore became the holder of the Wimbledon Laurels for the first time and was the London Riders' Champion. He had also been victorious in the Brandonapolis and was Irish Champion for the third successive year.

Holding off the young pretender, Jack Young was now being spoken of as a candidate for the greatest rider ever to race across the face of the planet. However, another contender for that title was rising in the north. Ove Fundin first took to the track in 1952, making a modest start with his first local Swedish team, Filbyternia. At that time ,Sweden were a second-rate speedway nation; in the not-too-distant future, Ove would help to transform his nation into a world speedway power.

As the season ticked over, Peter Craven had shared ten league outings equally between Liverpool and Belle Vue. He stayed with Liverpool for nearly two seasons and, after a brief spell with Fleetwood, moved permanently to Belle Vue in 1953. He started as a reserve, but quickly worked his way into the team.

Johnnie Hoskins moved on to Belle Vue in 1953. Charles Ochiltree took over at West Ham and Ken Brett filled in as speedway manager at the start of the season, until Tiger Stevenson took over. A second life was tragically claimed by the West Ham track in as many years when Harry Eyre, a twenty-four-year-old, died after crashing on 6 July 1953.

A beer and a bath, Howdy Byford, Jack Young and Wally Green, 1952.

Left: *A young Ove Fundin in patriotic mood.* Right: *Coalhole Keith Gurtner came to West Ham from New Cross in the early 1950s.*

'Swedish Swashbuckler' Ove Fundin in 1956.

The Hammers were really Jack Young this season. He topped the League averages with 10.3. The next highest West Ham average was Wally Green with 6.6. In many sides, this would have given him a ranking nearer to fifth place. If Green had been a Harringay rider with the same score, he would have come in at six in the club rankings. However, Pat Clarke showed some promising form early on in the season and his average went up by something like 2 points per match. But he was unable to keep up his form for the whole season. Craven, Byford and Curtis slumped badly.

The Hammers had signed Bert Roger (after his former club, New Cross, folded in mid-season) and Keith Gurtner, but neither of them made much of a mark. Norwegian Basse Hveem might have given Young some support, but he was injured after riding in only four matches and was out for the rest of the season. The *Daily Express*'s speedway correspondent, Basil Storey, appeared to get it right when he argued that: 'Howdy Byford, Keith Gurtner and Cliff Watson disappeared down the same coalhole as Green, Craven and, eventually, Clarke. And they took Bert Roger with them.'

It was only Young that kept West Ham viable, and it was almost totally down to him that the Hammers reached sixth place in the League. Knocked out in the fourth round (the first round West Ham entered) of the modified National Trophy, the team's solitary high point was reaching the final of the London Cup, beating Wimbledon in the last four. Out of character for the season, the East Londoners put up a real fight in the final, but in the end they were narrowly beaten by Harringay, 110-106.

Young continued to prosper on his own, defending his Match Race title against his old foe, Freddie Williams, and he again come out on top in a confrontation with Split Waterman. He gave up the title undefeated. At Wimbledon, he went on to win the Laurels and then made the London Riders' Championship his. Young grabbed more maximums than any other rider in the League and was picked by the Australian selectors for all three Test matches. He scored 17, 12 and 15 against the English to become his country's top scorer.

Young was favourite to retain his World Championship title, qualifying behind Ronnie Moore – who became a naturalised New Zealander that year – and Olle Nygren. Heat five was the critical conflict. Young faced Moore and Freddie Williams. Like heat six of 1952, Young found himself well adrift of Williams early on, but this time Jack had to settle for second place. However, the race seemed to take the best out of Williams, and he was defeated by Jeff Lloyd in the thirteenth heat.

This provided Young with a second bite at the proverbial cherry. Predictably, Young's gating was his downfall. The same problem plagued his following ride. Split Waterman, Dick Bradley and Eric Williams all left him standing. Three laps into the race, he caught Bradley. He burned through Williams in the last lap, but Waterman had got away. Williams won his final race and this was enough to deny Young a place in history as the only three-time winner of the world title. In his last outing of the contest, Young succumbed to the greasy track and fell. He finished with 10 points and fifth place. Freddie Williams became the second man to win the world crown twice. Moore scored 9 points for sixth place.

It was a somewhat ignominious end to what had previously been an almost flawless season for Young. Perhaps this was his provocation to seek a move away from Custom House. He reasoned that the track, because of its large size, tested a driver's capacity for speed and in so doing did not favour the skilful man. Young was almost certainly more skilful than any of his contemporaries and, this being the case, he felt that he needed a track whereon he might better deploy his talent. In an effort to retain Young, the West Ham management offered to shorten the 440-yard track by 25 yards. To the relief of everyone involved with the Hammers, this was enough to persuade Young stay true to the claret and blue.

Meanwhile, Ove Fundin, the pencil-slim Swede, had given up a career as a furrier to become a speedway rider. This began to pay off when he started to emerge as a world prospect in 1953 during a tour of England with his Filbyternia team-mates. At the same time, Barry Briggs was improving steadily at Wimbledon and, after help from his team-mate and fellow New Zealander, Ronnie Moore, was selected for the New Zealand side to face England in 1953.

9

THE ROAR IS SUCCEEDED
BY SILENCE

The Pits

*This is an area which is exclusive for the use of riders and officials. Regulations neces-
sitate that there is sufficient covered accommodation for the riders so that they can
work on their machines in inclement weather, and it must also be of sufficient size to
enable everyone to carry on their work without difficulty. In the pits there is usually
a fuel and oil store where the riders draw their supplies for the meeting and a first aid
room, in addition to workshops and equipment store. The dressing rooms – which
must be fitted with hot water showers sufficient in number to accommodate all the
riders properly – are usually situated in or near the pit area.*
Silver, L. 'Anatomy of a Speedway' in *The Speedway Annual* compiled by Silver, L. and
Douglas, P. (London, Pelham Books, 1969)

In 1954, West Ham found a rider to give Jack Young a hand. Gerald Hussey stared riding
at the Hertfordshire club, Rye House. His debut for the Hammers was as a reserve and
he did well, gaining 7 points for his side. Hussy progressed by degrees, despite picking
up an injury to his leg. In a World Championship qualifying round at West Ham, Hussey
defeated former Custom House idol Aub Lawson, Ronnie Moore and Tommy Price. In
the process, he recorded the fastest time of the night. He was on the verge of gaining
a reserve place in the Championship, but needed to beat Freddie Williams in a run-off.
However, this asked too much of the young rider and it was Williams who got the place.

The Hammers finished in the bottom half of the table: in the eight-team League they
came fifth. Green, Roger and Byford did not improve on their performances of the
previous season. Malcolm Craven had retired from the sport. The silver lining was
inevitably provided by Jack Young who, for the second year running, took the London
Riders' Championship. In the World Championship Final, he was a keen favourite to
win the title. There had been no one stronger than Jack in qualification. Of the possible
30 points, Young dropped only 1. In the sixth heat, he took to the track with three of
the strongest riders in the final: Ronnie Moore, Brian Crutcher and Aub Lawson.

A crash at Natestved in Denmark midway through the 1954 season had left Moore
with a leg in plaster and his knee broken in five places. After two months out of action,
a track return saw Moore qualify for his fifth World Final, despite the handicap of a still

mending leg. On World Final night itself, he was obliged to wear a metal brace to support his injured knee.

Moore blasted off as the tapes flew up and Crutcher burnt after him. Young, making his usual tardy response to the gate, captured Crutcher with little effort. It was then that a fracas of epic proportions commenced. Jack hit the Wembley whiz kid with all the weapons in his considerable armoury. But Ronnie was not there just for the ride; he fought back like a lion, throwing Young every which way, holding off the Antipodean enigma on the final straight to take the line as victor. Young, as in the previous year, was effectively beaten at the very beginning of the race. At the final count, he had to content himself with fourth place from his 11 points. Moore finished the final with a five-ride maximum to take his first world title from Brian Crutcher and Olle Nygren. It was a truly heroic effort. This was to be his outstanding performance in a fine year that saw Moore as club captain lead Wimbledon to the National League title for the first time in their history and to victory in the RAC Cup. The young Kiwi was beginning to look unstoppable.

However, a strong wind was blowing in from the mountains of New Zealand. This would grow to a tornado in the years to come. 1954 saw the World Championship debut of Barry Briggs. He was just twenty years of age and finished in a creditable fifth place with 9 points. Ove Fundin was also present at that Wembley final. Although last in the list of the sixteen finalists, with only 2 points, he had competed on a bike that was virtually homemade, painted fire-engine red. Peter Craven also qualified for his first World Final at Wembley in 1954 and scored 3 points, finishing in fifteenth place, just above Ove.

Fundin spent the winter in Australia, gaining more experience, and it was there that Aub Lawson and Jack Parker were quick to see potential of the young Swede. Lawson recommended Ove to his British team, Norwich. On his return from Australia, Fundin linked up with the East Anglian side in 1955. The experience he gained riding regularly in Britain paid handsome dividends.

A large cinder track that had been constructed at the rear of the Custom House stadium began to be used by West Ham in 1954. It was a venue for pushbike speedway, but an arrangement was made with West Ham's reserves, who used the track for training, for the Becton and Welling Amateur Speedway Club to store their machines there and get assistance with the maintenance of them. Vic Duffy and Harry Hassan formed the club in 1954 and it recruited members from West Essex, Kent, Woolwich and the Bexley Cycle Speedway League. This was another example of West Ham making innovative moves to attract local talent to its doors.

Meanwhile, Peter Craven was managing to combine his commitments racing for Belle Vue with his National Service. During 1954, he made 24 league appearances and topped the score chart for the big northern club with 200 points for an average of 8.3 points per meeting. His thrilling balance-defying style came to the notice of the England selectors and he rode three times for his country.

West Ham finished bottom of the League the following year, and this is when Jack Young appeared to think that enough was enough and that he could go nowhere with

West Ham, 1955. From left to right: Cliff Watson, Kid Curtis, Reg Fearman, Frank Bettis, Malcolm Craven, George Wilks, Aub Lawson, Howdy Byford, Wally Green (sitting on the ground).

a team that lacked the ambition to provide him with adequate support. The Hammers seemed, as much as anything else, to have a problem with morale. Looking at the team roster, the side looked more solid than it had for half a decade. When Harringay resigned from the League, Split Waterman and Jack Biggs were brought to Custom House, and that gave West Ham, with Wally Green and Gerry Hussey, a fistful of internationals. This group were supported by the potentially strong Bert Roger and Alan Smith. So, at the start of 1955, Young should have had a team around him rather than a side that hung around him. However, whilst West Ham had the bricks, the mortar seemed to be missing. Young, as was usual by now, was number one in the scoring charts, averaging more than 11 points a match. Unfortunately, this achievement was cancelled out by Waterman's lowly 6.76 and Hussey's poor 6.43. The remaining riders were even more pitiful. The National Trophy saw the Hammers defeated by Norwich: the East Anglians pulverising the East Enders 127-88 in the first round.

The West Ham miasma had begun to affect Young's individual performances. A disappointing third place in the London Riders' Championship was followed by a disastrous first race in the World Championship in which he was humbled, trailing in behind Eric Williams and Billy Bales. This effectively ended his chances from the outset. In stark contrast, Ronnie Moore had another fine year in 1955. With 12 points he finished runner-up in the World Final to Peter Craven. Moore had again fought out the final despite injury. He arrived at Wembley with a broken collarbone. He also held the British Match Race Championship for a period, and successfully led the Dons to a second successive National League title. At the end of the season, he decided to give racing cars a go, an enthusiasm that stayed with him for a couple of years. As the season concluded with a pathetic 'phut' at Custom House, Young let it be known that he would not return from Australia in 1956 and that he wanted to be with his family and to have some time to watch his children grow up – something that he had not been able to do when carrying the entire West Ham side as his pillion passengers.

Everyone at West Ham knew that this was the end. They had lost one of the best riders on Earth and could not hope to replace him. The management were fully aware that the crowds would not turn up after the loss of the team's star – and effectively its only rider for the last few seasons. Gates had slumped anyway, relative to the glory days of the late 1940s and early 1950s. The last drop of West Ham 'dope' had been used up at Custom House and so speedway pulled into the pits in the East End of London. It would be nine years before it rolled back onto the track.

Speedway went into extended hibernation in Custom House at the end of the 1955 campaign, partly due to West Ham's poor performances (that were arguably a consequence of the team's uninspired management), but also as a symptom of the general demise of speedway in Britain during the mid-1950s. By 1955, the number of spectators that the sport was attracting had fallen dramatically from that of the immediate post-war boom years. Many reasons for the slump can be suggested. Perhaps the sport had expanded too quickly after the Second World War and left itself open to a sudden falling away of interest. It was, of course, also the period of 'telemania', with many people finding entertainment brought to them in their own homes for the first time.

Gerry Hussey going into the turn.

Wheels On Fire

Much of the thrill had gone out of speedway racing. It had become somewhat proces-sional, with riders widely spaced out; the excitement of close racing was fading and tracks were closing all over the country. This was related to the pattern of riders passing through the sport. For the first five years after the Second World War, team places were generally filled by riders who had ridden before the hostilities broke out – such as Bill Kitchen, Tommy Price, Jack and Norman Parker and Oliver Hart, with only a few vacancies left in the First Division. The few younger riders who did find First Division places, such as Ronnie Moore and Barry Briggs, although outclassed initially, became very accomplished by the mid-1950s.

Many of the pre-war riders did not return to the sport with the advent of peace – more than a few had reached the age of speedway retirement during the war. The old guard was further diminished in the early 1950s, but their places were filled by novices who were simply unable to match riders like Moore and Briggs. The consequence was that many races became all too predictable. A means of slowing down the faster riders to create closer racing was produced by a rule change in 1956. The consequence of this was that whilst the front wheel, which was much narrower than the leading tyre of a road bike, would remain the same, the rear knobbly tyre was outlawed and the Dunlop Trials Universal tyre became the only legitimate racing tyre. The latter had similar block pattern tread to the ordinary road bike tyre of the day, albeit slightly deeper. The size of the rear tyre of a race bike would now be 350 x 19. This affected the gripping power of the speedway machine detrimentally.

However, the speedway riders of the 1950s, and their advisors from earlier days, were an inventive group. As soon as they were obliged to use the different tyres, they started to cut the tread blocks, widening the spaces between, and cutting at as much of an angle as the tread blocks would allow. This simulated the angled bands of the former tyres. Reducing the tread blocks shortened the life of the tyres, but this, again, gave an advantage to those whose earnings enabled more frequent tyre renewals. The rules had to be re-written again and cut tyres became illegal. In due course, a new, 19in-diameter standard speedway regulation tyre was put into production, together with the ruling of one new edge per meeting.

The wheel-size rule change may well have had an economic motivation as well. Prior to the rule change, the rear tyres had to be made specially. Apart from Dunlop, only a small privately-owned operation, which was more popular with the riders, made the speedway tyres. With the demise of speedway, Dunlop decided not to continue with the manufacture of what, to them, was a very limited sale item. This left the small inde-pendent company as the sole manufacturer of suitable tyres. For them, speedway tyre production could only be operated on a small batch basis, so they decided to increase their profit margin on the special original speedway tyre. This resulted in many less successful riders being unable to afford the specialist tyres. Newer riders, those generally at the back of the competition processions, were not earning much from their point-scoring and could not afford to invest in their bikes, and keep their machines as well-tuned as they might. Such was the cost of racing that one Wimbledon rider, for example, was reputed to have had to make use of a 'float' motor-cycle sidecar outfit to get himself and his bike to meetings, no longer able to afford car and trailer. However, those riders with more experience and earnings could afford new tyres for each meeting and as such maintain the extra speed.

The Speedway Riders' Association (SRA) – which is a kind of trade union for speedway riders – asked the manufacturer to give a written undertaking not to significantly increase the price of their tyres. The company were unable to agree to this request. As such, the SRA held a meeting and decided to bring their wheel size into line with normal motorcycles so that they could use a mass-produced trials tyre. As a result, the wheel size remained at 19in.

This being the case, the wheel-size rule could be understood as an attempt to 'level the playing field' (or track) economically. By accident or design, the sport was, in practice, supporting its roots, that were very much set in the working class culture. Whatever the motivation of the wheel-size rule, the overall effect of this activity was that the number of motorcade-type races were reduced, but not to the extent needed to bring the crowds back.

The Times They Are A-changing (To Russia With Love)

Another blow to the prestige of speedway was the disappearance of international events between Britain and Australia, which lapsed in the late 1950s (Australian speedway went into a much more profound decline than was being experienced in Britain). Now out of an Army uniform, in September 1955, Peter Craven won the World Championship final at Wembley in September to become the second Englishman to take the title – and it was only his second attempt!

There were also signs that the geographical centre of speedway was shifting. This was becoming apparent in the mid-1950s with the emergence of Olle Nygren and Ove Fundin; Sweden was beginning to take the sport seriously. Fundin had become a stylish rider and dominated the speedways in the late 1950s and early 1960s. 'The Fox' was to become one of the giants of speedway racing. A combination of tenacity, temperament and talent carried him to the very top in the sport. His nickname was derived from his flaming red hair. He was to win the supreme individual title five times. He stood on the World Final rostrum for ten consecutive years following his first title win in 1956, when he became the first continental rider to take the Championship, having kept Ronnie Moore in second again on 12 points.

A month or so after the World Final, Ove married Mona Forsberg. The couple met when both were schoolchildren in their hometown of Tranas, Sweden. They courted from their earliest teenage years, and Ove always promised his sweetheart that they would marry when he became World Speedway Champion. Mona placed her faith in Ove, and Ove's love for Mona was always a motivation as he pursued sporting excellence on the oval tracks of the world.

The New Zealanders were also becoming a major force on the international scene with the rise of Barry Briggs and Ronnie Moore. In 1956, apart from being runner-up in the World Championship, Moore took the New Zealand Championship for the first time and won his second Wimbledon Laurels. He achieved further success in the British Match Race Championship. However, the thrill of the speedway was beginning to lose its magic and at the end of 1956, Ronnie retired from the sport to concentrate on successfully racing Cooper cars, which caused him to miss the 1957 season, including the World Championships, and the best part of 1958. With Moore out of the running, Barry Briggs won his first World Championship title in 1957. It had been a good couple of years for him, having also got married the previous year.

In 1956, another Christchurch New Zealander was starting out on a speedway career. He made the World Championship his goal from the moment he first watched Norman Parker ride with the English tourists on his local track. Like so many boys, his first two-wheeled speedway was on a cycle. He won just about everything to be won in this discipline on the South Island before taking to the motorised sport. He recalled: 'With my youthful ego, I said to myself, this speedway lark is easy, I could do it too. So I got myself a bike, and had a go. Like most sports viewed from the terracing, speedway racing looks easy done by experts. But I soon found out that it wasn't.'

Ivan Mauger (pronounced 'major') was of French extraction, his grandfather having moved from Jersey to New Zealand. He had been a schoolboy athlete of some distinction when he first took to the dirt track, although he was not an instant success. He came to Britain on honeymoon in 1957 as a seventeen-year-old and decided to try his luck with Walthamstow, where Moore and Briggs had first hit the dirt-tracks of Britain. However, he found little success in the old Southern Area Sunday Afternoon League, nor in occasional second-half outings at Wimbledon. By the end of the year, he was on his way home, realising that he had a lot to learn before he could make the big-time.

A further sign of speedway's increasing international profile came in 1958, when Moscow staged the USSR's first speedway meeting.

All these considerations gave little comfort to the lovers of West Ham speedway and oval racing in general on 6 September 1955: this was the date when speedway stopped at Custom House, something even Hitler and the Luftwaffe had failed to completely accomplish. Symbolically perhaps, in the final event before the closure of West Ham, Barry Briggs won the Stadium Cup.

Although speedway looked to be dying at a domestic level, England was still holding its own on the international front. In 1958, Peter Craven captained the English team against Sweden in Sweden, finishing as top scorer in the three-Test series; he also topped the score chart in the five-Test series against Australasian (a combined Australian and New Zealand team), scoring 73 points. After scoring 11 points, Peter was involved in a run-off for third position at the World Final, again at Wembley. He fell but remounted to finish fourth overall. Ronnie Moore, who had found the lure of the speedway too great and had returned to the sport in June 1958, despite having the handicap of taking to the track months after his rivals, was still good enough to qualify for his eighth World Final. However, he finished in a disappointing seventh place with 9 points, watching his compatriot, team-mate and protégé Barry Briggs retain the title and score a maximum 15 points in the process. Before the Championship bikes had

Barry Briggs (Swindon) receiving the Golden Helmet Match Race Championship from Don Clarke of The Sunday Mirror. *Tommy Price (West Ham manager) looks on in awe.*

cooled, Briggs, perhaps emulating his guru, announced his retirement. Moore, however, went on to help Wimbledon regain the National League title that they had lost during his absence.

Following the closure of West Ham, many assumed that speedway itself was dying, and this looked possible when, after the death of Sir Arthur Elvin, a long-time friend of speedway, Wembley followed West Ham and closed down in 1956. Through the years the sport, which had at one time boasted first, second and third divisions, had slowly become depleted. By 1959, speedway had slumped to a mere one division and nine tracks. In London, once the home of top-flight teams, only Wimbledon survived as a big club. Barry Briggs couldn't resist the pull of the track, and returned to defend his title. Ironically, perhaps, he wasn't able to overcome Ronnie Moore on this occasion.

Without the perseverance of the nine tracks that held on through the bitter years of the speedway recession, it is doubtful that the sport would be alive in Britain today. Speedway did survive – but only just – aided by the likes of Peter Craven, who had a typical season in 1959. In 81 meetings, he amassed a total of 1,099 points from 428 races. He was back at Wembley for the World Final, but he suffered from bad gating and track bumps also caused him problems. He finished the meeting with only 7 points. However, that year he took on Ove Fundin and won the Golden Helmet Match Race Championship and the Champions of Champions Cup at Poole. He was also victorious in the Northern Cup at Belle Vue, the Internationale Derby at Ipswich, the Pride of the East at Norwich, the Tom Farndon Memorial Trophy at New Cross, the Champagne Derby, again at Belle Vue, the CTS Trophy at Norwich, and the Pride of the Midlands, at Leicester.

Ronnie Moore reassumed his role as team captain of Wimbledon and led his side to a clean sweep of honours with yet another League Championship, victory in the National Trophy and an easy win over Belle Vue in the final of the Britannia Shield. At Southampton, he won the Billy Butlin Trophy. A second World title triumph at Wembley in front of almost 70,000 fans crowned Ronnie's season. He rode to an immaculate 15-point maximum to take the title ahead of Ove Fundin and Barry Briggs, despite carrying torn ligaments and a broken bone in his foot.

In 1960, traces of a silver lining appeared in the speedway cloud of desperation. A group of enthusiasts, some of them former riders, linked up to form the Provincial League. Old tracks were revived and new tracks introduced. In a matter of months, the number of speedway tracks in Britain more than doubled. Although Australian interest in speedway continued to decline, the scene in Europe was improving. Swedish speedway was thriving, and Poland, Czechoslovakia and the USSR were coming into the picture. This culminated in 1960, when international competition received a great fillip with the introduction of the World Team Cup.

This was to be another good year for 'Miracle' Moore. He started the season by defeating Peter Craven to again win the British Match Race Championship. Further success came with a second Brandonapolis Championship and wins in the Tom Farndon Memorial Trophy at New Cross, the Laurels at Wimbledon and the Kings of Oxford at the Cowley raceway. On the team front, Wimbledon successfully defended their National League and National Trophy titles.

Belle Vue and England skipper Peter Craven produced what was to be perhaps his finest performance in 1960, when he led England in an international series in Poland. While most of the English team found the Polish conditions difficult to master, Craven scored 59 points in three matches, including 21-point maximums in two of the meetings. Back home, he was in devastating form. Track records fell all over the place, and he picked up many individual honours whilst successfully representing his country in Test matches. He again finished as the highest British scorer in qualifying for the World Final. On the night of the Wembley event, Peter was involved in a triple run-off for first place, with Ronnie Moore and Ove Fundin – all had scored 14 points. Still recovering from an earlier spill, the best Peter could manage was third, behind the winner Fundin, who led from the gate to finishing line, shrugging off Moore's attempts to power past him.

Both Moore and Craven were now established in the top five riders in speedway, which would probably also have included Barry Briggs. He had ridden for New Cross until the end of the 1960 season and then moved to Southampton, who paid a £750 transfer fee for his services – an astronomical sum by speedway standards of that period.

During 1961, Craven captained the Lions on a tour to Austria. He was third in the first International Individual Championship meeting (held on only one occasion) at Harringay. He was second in the British Final at Wembley, which was won by Barry Briggs. The little scouser went on that season to finish second in the Laurels at Wimbledon. He won the Pride of the South and the Pride of the Midlands. He was also victorious in the Pride of the East, the Kings of Oxford Trophy at Oxford and was runner-up in the Tom Farndon Memorial Trophy at New Cross.

By 1961, the organisation and the site of the World Championship had changed. Wembley had long been synonymous with the World Championship, but with the overseas boom in speedway, it came as no surprise when the FIM (Federation Internationale Motorcycliste), the ruling body of all two-wheeled sport, gave the event to another country. Sweden staged the first World Final outside Britain (and Wembley) at Mälmo, and the home nation achieved only the third 1-2-3. It was largely due to Ove Fundin that the speedway World Final was staged outside England for the first time in 1961. He led the Swedish clean sweep, followed in by his fellow countrymen, Bjorn Knutsson and Gote Nordin. Craven fell in his first ride and finished with a disappointing total of 6 points. Ronnie Moore ended up just above him in fifth with a 10-point score.

Moore led his Wimbledon side to their seventh League Championship in eight seasons and to a London Cup victory against New Cross. Individually, he secured the Gold Cup Championship at Wimbledon. On the other side of the planet, Ivan Mauger won in the 1961 Victorian Championships in Australia, beating the former World

The first three to finish in the World Speedway Final of 1960 – Ove Fundin, Ronnie Moore and Peter Craven.

Champion, Jack Young, who had for so long been his idol, twice in the process. Despite all his subsequent success, he rated this achievement as a high point in his career. It coincided with the birth of his third daughter, Debbie. She joined one-year-old Kim and Julie, who was three at the time, in the Mauger household.

1962 was another vintage Craven year. He followed his three rounds of British Championship victories by notching up 14 points to carry off the World Individual Championship, now back at Wembley. He had made ten successive World Final appearances, and had won the title for a second time, the first Englishman to accomplish this feat. For a time, it looked as if Ronnie Moore might have been heading for his third World Championship when he won his first two rides. However, in his third race, when challenging Craven, Ronnie's fuel tank came adrift and his hopes of a third title went with it. He finished seventh with 9 points.

Craven topped the National League points chart, won the Kings of Oxford Trophy again, was third in the Internationale and took the runner-up spot in the Pride of the East at Norwich. Riding with Gerald Jackson, Craven also won the Best Pairs event at Wimbledon.

In 1962, the Big Five of the track – Ronnie Moore, Ove Fundin, Peter Craven, Bjorn Knutsson and Barry Briggs (who was to help Southampton win the National League Championship that season) – were handicapped in league racing by being made to start twenty yards back from the others. However, it made little difference and Moore still headed the Wimbledon point-scorers at the end of the season. Wimbledon finished as runners-up in the League to Southampton, but it was a another successful year for the Dons as Ronnie led them to victories against Swindon in the National Trophy and Coventry in the Knockout Cup. Moore concluded the season by defeating Ove Fundin in a sensational run-off at Wimbledon for the Gold Cup. After being some distance behind as the last lap started, he took the final bend fast and wide, then, on reaching the apex of the turn, he cut back to the inside of the track to squeeze past Fundin to take the victory.

During the slump years of the late 1950s and early 1960s, Ron Wilson, a rider at Leicester, was blessed with a son, Raymond. Born in Merton, Surrey, little Ray would do much to bring speedway back into the light one day. He took his first ride on the Leicester track in mid-1962, when the 'Hunters', as they were then, were in the Provincial League. It was an after-the-meeting outing, under his dad's watchful eye. But his riding would be limited for a while to occasional trips to 'Sunday school' at Rye House training track, until Ray had passed his O-levels at the Beaumont Lees Secondary School.

10
REVVING RENAISSANCE

The Fuel And Oil Man

As his name indicates, this staff member is responsible for issuing to the riders their requirements in fuel and oil. He must carefully measure each pint or gallon issued for both of these items are very expensive, the fuel being methanol costing up to 12s per gallon and the racing oil anything up to 7s 6d per pint. He must obtain a signature from each rider as he issues the fuel on a form provided by the management, and from this form the manager deducts the cost of the fuel taken from the rider's pay cheque. An important part of his job is to keep the management informed of the amount of supplies in hand, and many meetings have been in jeopardy when fuel supplies have run short through an inefficient fuel and oil man.
Silver, L. 'Vital Cogs' in *The Speedway Annual* compiled by Silver, L. and Douglas, P. (London, Pelham Books, 1969)

As World Champion at the start of the 1963 season, Peter Craven was automatically selected as the challenger for the Golden Helmet Match Race title. He had already won the event on several occasions, but at this point it was held by his old rival, Ove Fundin. Craven finally defeated Fundin, at the usual neutral track decider, after both won one leg each. Peter then successfully defended the title against Barry Briggs, but lost it to Fundin in mid-season.

As British Champion and top qualifier, Craven was again at Wembley in 1963 for the World Championship final, but he didn't ride particularly well. A few days later, he rode in the Gold Cup final at Wimbledon, scoring 10 points and finishing joint sixth with Ove Fundin. Seventy-two hours later, he was at Norwich where he only managed to score 7 points.

Following the Wednesday outing in East Anglia on the Friday night, just a week after the 1963 World Final, he was racing for Belle Vue in a challenge match against the Provincial League champions, Edinburgh. After three brilliant wins, he crashed heavily in his fourth outing, smashing into a safety fence after trying to avoid a fallen rider. He succumbed to serious head injuries a few days later. Craven was at the peak of his career; with his death, Britain lost its most consistent post-war rider and its only really serious challenger to the foreign and overseas domination of the speedway.

It is easy to watch riders pound around tracks and take their safety for granted. The fan puts a lot of faith in the skill of the man in the saddle and the soundness of his mount. But the thrill of speedway is connected to the danger involved: the potential for disaster is an element of the sport's attraction. Quite how much the viewing fan, who is involved in looking rather than doing, wants to confront this fact is questionable. Certainly, most riders, at some level, must at some time be aware that their own neck being on the line is part of the entertainment. There is something of the gladiatorial spectacle in this. However, the aesthetic of speedway takes precedence over its more ghoulish potential.

Peter Craven's name was perpetuated in speedway by a memorial trophy meeting that was staged annually at Belle Vue. He was survived by a wife and two children.

Peter Craven's World Championship Record
* maximum possible points: 15
+ after run-off for 1st place

Year	Venue	Points*	Position
1954	Wembley	3	15th
1955	Wembley	13	1st
1956	Wembley	11	4th
1957	Wembley	11	4th
1958	Wembley	11	4th
1959	Wembley	7	8th
1960	Wembley	14	3rd+
1961	Malmo	6	10th
1962	Wembley	14	1st
1963	Wembley	6	10th

By 1963, there were two divisions in Britain, but only six tracks in the top flight. In the face of a deep crisis a group of promoters, headed by Charles Ochiltree, organised themselves into an alliance in an effort to revitalise speedway in the British context and created the National League.

This year was to be Ronnie 'Mirac' Moore's last season in British speedway for some time. Initially, it looked as if it was going to be another great campaign, as Ronnie posted victories in the Malcolm Flood Memorial Meeting held at Norwich and the London Cup at Wimbledon. The latter was a repeat of the 1962 victory in the Gold Cup, with Ronnie having to overpower Ove Fundin in a run-off. As they shrieked into the final lap, Moore was a long way behind – like the previous year, he again ran out extremely wide on the last bend of the race. The Swede, sensing his opponent's intentions to again try and cut back up the inside, adhered himself to the white, but 'Mirac' held the taps on hard, sustaining the pressure on the outside line at full throttle, giving himself the extra velocity. The combatants shot over the line as one, but Fundin had been beaten.

In the final heat of the match between Wimbledon and Swindon, on 20 May in the National League, Moore, racing off his twenty-yard handicap, ploughed into Bob Andrews and Martin Ashby, who had taken falls in front of him. Ronnie's bike fell on his left leg from a great height and it snapped just above the ankle. Moore would not recover fitness that season and, after he had attended a benefit meeting held for him at the end of the term, he announced his retirement and returned to New Zealand to concentrate on the less demanding 'wall of death' business. Since his first World Final, he had appeared in twelve of them in the following thirteen years.

Ronnie was persuaded to return to action one more time to ride against his old Wimbledon team-mate and brother-in-law, Geoff Mardon. Encouraged by his performance, he started to ride the Templeton track on a casual basis.

As one great New Zealander's thoughts turned to home shores, a future giant of the speedways came the other way. Ivan Mauger had spent three seasons on the tracks of his homeland, gaining two titles before concentrating on the Australia scene, where the dark-haired, wiry 5ft 6in Kiwi dominated, taking numerous state titles. He was now ready for Britain and in 1963 he accepted an invitation to ride for Newcastle in the Provincial League. He was an instant success and won the Provincial Riders' Championship in 1963 and 1964. He was only deprived of a hat-trick by the formation of the British League.

Under the hand of Charles Ochiltree, West Ham was reopened by the National League promoters and the speedway roar returned to Custom House in 1964. Tommy Price was team manager and promoter.

In the post-war years, the Provincial League had kept speedway on the sporting map. However, in 1964, a number of the newer Provincial League clubs mutinied against the Speedway Control Board (SCB) and continued to function, even though they lacked the appropriate licence. As a consequence of this, any rider riding in Provincial League meetings would risk having his licence revoked by the ACU.

Malcolm Simmons, a top grass-track rider in the south of England, could not take the chance of losing his licence. He had spent 1963 with Hackney in the National League but rode for Rayleigh, a Provincial League club, during their Good Friday contest. After an appeal by Simmons, he was told that his licence would not be affected if he joined the National League. Tommy Price signed him for West Ham in May, feeling that the eighteen-year-old had the makings of a fine speedway rider.

One of Price's first signings had been the Swedish star, Bjorn Knutsson, whom he immediately made skipper of the side and, on Tuesday 7 April, the Hammers defeated Wimbledon 46-38 in a challenge match witnessed by a claret-and-blue adorned crowd of 15,000. The team included: Knutsson, Stan Stevens, Norman Hunter, Reg Luckhurst, Alf Hagon and Bobby Dugard. Brian Brett and the great Barry Briggs guested for West Ham. Knutsson achieved maximum points for his side.

Restoration And Remembrance

A handful of weeks into the West Ham renaissance, a few hundred yards from the giant cranes of the East India Dock, local kids could again stand in the street on Tuesday evenings and watch the riders arriving with their bikes strapped on the back of their cars and hear the revving of engines from within the stadium. Groups of merchant seamen, fidgeting in their shore clothes, stared at the neon-lit Custom House Stadium. They hung about on street corners around the arena, listening to the cacophony of noise that the tight communities nestling around the cockney oval of speed were again learning to make part of their lives. Loudspeakers blared out pop music amidst the grumbling snarl of straining machines. This fusion of noise was itself engulfed by the rumble and roar of the West Ham horde as they pushed their side on a wind of sound, punctuated by such chants as: '2, 4, 6, 8 – Who do we appreciate? H-A-M-M-E-R-S … Hammers!' This loop of resonance started at eight o'clock and continued for over two hours. It proclaimed that speedway was back, north of the river, east of the Tower.

At this time, speedway was still a rough-and-tumble sport, so the speedway rider had to kit himself out accordingly. As well as encasing himself in leather and a crash helmet, he usually wore both goggles and face visor for protection from falls and churned-up dust. His left boot did a lot of work on corners, so he clipped a steel sole onto it. The machine he rode was in a class of its own, probably the purest and most basic racing machine. Anyone taking one of these powerful motorcycles on the road would face prosecution. It had a clutch and a throttle, but no breaks, no rear suspension and only one gear, although this could be adjusted to various conditions and tracks. The purpose-built frame housed a single-cylinder, four-stroke, methanol-burning 500cc racing engine. It had a tremendous power-to-weight ratio and was capable of going from 0 to 60 mph in around three seconds, with a potential top-end speed in the region of 140 mph. It looked mean and menacing, and it was just that, leaving no one with any doubts about its purpose – to ride fast and hard and win. It was more a racing weapon than a means of getting from 'A' to 'B'.

It was on corners that speedway reputations were made or broken. Top riders could work their way from third place to first in two laps by getting through corners: first they would drift, then roar sharply into the straight. According to West Ham's Alf Hagon in 1964: 'You have to throw your bike into the corner flat. You have to throw your bike into the corner – you just rely on the skidding to slow you down.' Cornering speed was about 40 mph, while on the straight the bikes would reach up to 60 mph.

At this time, some of the riders at West Ham were new to the sport, others could recall the golden days just after the war; most of them were wise enough to recognise that speedway, like all things in life, is subject to the ebb and flow of existence, fate and fancy. Alf Hagon had been riding professionally for a decade. He began his career in the saddle at Harringay, moving on to Wimbledon, then Leicester and Oxford, before eventually arriving on his home turf at Custom House. Like many riders before him, he was recognised by young fans, his face was that of the smiling hero that looked out at them from on the front cover of the match programme. They often ran up for his autograph.

After his fourth race, he sat astride his bike sipping tea from a paper cup. Hagon at this time would have described himself, unpretentiously, as a semi-professional. He knew that if he was lucky he could pick up £50 to £80 a week riding the tracks, a good wage in 1964. However, when he had started out, during the boom years, it was £100. Outside of racing, he ran a motorcycle shop in Leyton, a part of East London bordering Epping Forest – the birthplace of speedway. If riders wanted to, they could have ridden on a full-time basis. A few years before, Hagon had made his way to the other side of the world during the English speedway winter to compete in the Australian season. Although some of the boys still did that, summer riding was enough for Hagon come the mid-1960s.

He replaced the blue helmet on his head and again hid his features behind a leather mask before blasting off for his next contest. At the end of the first lap, Hagon seemed to be beaten, but some adventurous cornering cannoned him into second berth. In the final few feet of the last lap, he inched to the front of the pack, ripping three points from the race that converted into his purse and amounted to 67s 6d. An opponent had fallen from his bike on the first bend. He was hurt, but not badly in speedway terms. Hagon, coated in the fine brown mist of cinders, looked back down the track at the man being carried off, but as he saw it, playing football was more dangerous. Hagon's fellow Hammer, Mike Simmons, wore leathers that were still shining. His face looked even younger than his eighteen years. The previous season had been his first in speedway. He pulled in around £500, but this did not include income from his grass-track riding. As was common to all riders, Simmons had to maintain his own equipment. 1964 had not been a good year for him; mechanical problems with his bike had cost him dearly.

Neither Hagon nor Simmons were worried by the thought that speedway might eventually die out in Britain. They saw it as a fixed part of British culture. Hagon assumed it would just keep ticking over. Perhaps people were starting to come out in the evenings again.

Resolution And Rebuilding

Ray Cresp, formerly of Ipswich, and another Swede, the young Bengt Jansson, were added to the West Ham side. With Hunter, Luckhurst, Jansson and Simmons, the Hammers looked to be brimming with potential. However, Knutsson was the only automatic heat-leader and the team struggled, finishing the season propping up the rest of the League. Knutsson's average of 10.5 was more than respectable, but the nearest to him was Luckhurst with 6.08. West Ham were again looking dangerously like a one-rider team.

Thirty-three-year-old Swindon rider Tadeusz Teodorowicy crashed at Custom House on Tuesday 1 September. Following a fight for life that lasted 142 days, 'Teo' died without regaining consciousness in January 1965.

As the end of the season drew near, Jansson and Luckhurst gave some cause for optimism, helping the Hammers to reach the final of the National Trophy. They were unlucky, getting beaten by a mere 2 points by Oxford, the League Champions of that term. Jansson also showed his potential by taking the runner-up place in the restored London Riders' Championship.

Gothenburg's Ullevi Stadium staged the World Championship Final for the first time in 1964, and West Ham's Bjorn Knutsson scored 10 points in the event, pushing himself into fifth place. Many thought that he might one day become World Champion if he could find a way of controlling his nerves on the big occasion. He was to fly very high indeed after he moved away from Custom House. The Swedes were the accepted

Barry Briggs and pop star Alvin Stardust, Wimbledon, 1965.

masters of speedway at this time, but Barry Briggs turned in an outstanding performance to take the title with maximum points.

The World Championship wasn't the only battle Briggs had on his hands in 1964. Riding for Swindon, Briggs – along with Ove Fundin and Bjorn Knutsson – had been given a ten-yard handicap in every race. He successfully protested against this practice and from even starts had one of his best seasons. As well as winning his third World Championship, he was also victorious the FIM Internationale, the British Championship and the Golden Helmet Match Race Championship.

After ten magnificent seasons with Norwich, Ove Fundin left speedway, just before the track was sold for redevelopment at the end of 1964. His ruthless pursuit of success – no one hated to lose more than Fundin – often upset the British crowds, but at Norwich he was adored. His brilliance astride a speedway machine was not matched with technical knowledge; in terms of the mechanics of motorcycles, he was ignorant and never even owned a bike. Most tracks in those days had a spare machine for anyone to use and Fundin rode Norwich Track Spare No. 2. He sped to many a glorious victory on this machine and freely admitted that his ruthless determination to be, and remain, the very best made him hell to be around when he was racing. He once said: 'I had red hair, and red-haired people are aggressive and hot-tempered, which I certainly was. But you have got to be ruthless, and like in any individual sport you've got to be selfish. I am the first one to admit I am very selfish.' This attitude swept him to the pinnacle of his chosen sport. As well as his World titles, he was European Champion five times, Swedish Champion nine times and the first Swedish rider to top 1,000 points in internationals.

As seemed to be the way with speedway, as one giant left the sport there was another gifted rider waiting in the wings to take up the space vacated. It was in 1965, with the Long Eaton side in the new British League, that young Ray Wilson became a more subdued and relaxed rider. His fireball spirit was still there, but the apparent over-eagerness had been tempered. His head was beginning to govern his right hand and he was maturing well.

Towards the end of the year, the Royal Automobile Club set up an inquiry into speedway. Lord Shawcross chaired the process and eventually come out in favour of the Provincial League promoters. This led to the complete reorganisation of the sport. The inquiry concluded that the Provincial League and the seven-club National League should come together to create a British League. The following year, along with seventeen other clubs, West Ham became a founding member of the British League. The amalgamation brought the opportunity for changes to be made in the way speedway was organised. Promoters of the sport gained greater influence in terms of how speedway was to be administrated. The British Speedway Promoter's Association (BSPA) was established and given the job of organising domestic speedway in Britain. A reorganised Speedway Control Board was set-up with the power to reject or accept the recommendations and decisions made by the promoters. Overall, British speedway in the mid-1960s had a more effective and efficient structure in place than at any time in the past.

West Ham took the opportunity to rebuild around young Malcolm Simmons. Knutsson, having gone home to Sweden at the end of the previous season, chose not to come back to London. Reg Luckhurst, Ray Cresp, Bengt Jansson and Alf Hagon also all moved on. Norman Hunter and Bobby Dugard took their places, along with the Norwegian, Sverre Harrfeldt, from Wimbledon. Ken McKinlay, who had been captain of Leicester and Coventry also came to Custom House to lead the side. Australian Dave Wills and the young Ted Ede were two more new Hammers that season.

The season was still young when Bobby Dugard made his way to Wimbledon. Brian Leonard, the former Poole rider, was brought in. Reg Trott reinforced the side later that year, Reg's former club, Norwich, having disappeared off of the face of the planet.

British League Champions

The Hammers' supporters might well have felt confident about the coming season. The side had, in Harrfeldt and McKinlay, two recognised heat-leaders

Retiring president of the Veteran Speedway Riders' Association, Reg Fearman, hands over the chain of office to incoming president Ove Fundin in 1993.

Ted Ede and Terry Stone fighting for West Ham at Belle Vue.

and Hunter had scored 11 points in the first match against Wimbledon. But the 1965 campaign didn't start too well. May saw just two victories out of a possible nine. In June, the Hammers were barely able to pass a sad Newport side at Custom House in the Knockout Cup. Morale sunk to rock bottom when, on 22 June, Dave Wills tragically died in a smash in a match against Belle Vue. The accident happened in the second half of the contest.

At the start of August, in the next round of the cup, West Ham needed the gods on their side to achieve a draw with Wimbledon at Custom House. It took an engine explosion to save the match for West Ham, putting a Dons bike out in the final heat of the contest, to tie the match 48-48. However, the replay of 14 August saw the start of a dramatic turnaround in the Hammers' form. This was to be one of the most memorable and most thrilling contests West Ham had ever taken part in.

Wimbledon were hot favourites to beat the East Londoners on their own dirt, and it hardly seemed worthwhile for the West Ham side to make the trip across London when, adding to loss of Sverre Harfeldt, who had injured himself at Hackney on the day before the match, Norman Hunter, the Hammers' leading points taker, withdrew from the match to get married. A win for the Dons looked almost a certainty. Given the circumstances, there was no choice but to give rookie Tony Clarke a baptism of fire. Geoff Hughes took up the reserve berth. After half-a-dozen heats Wimbledon were on top 21-15. The next race scheduled Wimbledon men Keith Whipp and former Hammer

Bobby Dugard, who had won his first race, to face West Ham's Malcolm Simmons and Ray Wickett. However, a change in strategy meant that Ken McKinlay came in as a substitute for Wickett. Simmons tore over the line in front of the pack, giving West Ham a 5-1 score. Heat eight saw another 5-1 to West Ham. Brian Leonard came home first in the next race for a 3-3 and this was followed by another Simmons victory, leaving the Wimbledon captain, Olle Nygren, in his wake.

Heat twelve brought yet another 5-1 for West Ham, putting them 6 points up. Now it was Wimbledon's turn to make a tactical substitution. They slotted Olle Nygren into a pairing with Reg Luckhurst to face the West Ham duo of Simmons and Wickett. Undaunted, Simmons swept into the lead as the tape flew and stayed there. Heats fourteen and fifteen finished in a 5-1 and a 4-2 for the Dons. Now, with one heat to go, the points stood at 45-45. The deciding race saw Whipp and Luckhurst came to the line for Wimbledon. McKinlay and Simmons carried the claret and blue. Tension filled the air, but what was needed now was focus and cool heads. West Ham fans had seen their side come back from the grave of the first tie and now they watched in awe and suspended belief as Simmons powered home leaving Luckhurst floundering.

It was the West Ham man's fourth win of the night. McKinlay done his job by taking third place, giving a 4-2 heat score to West Ham and a 49-47 match triumph for the Hammers. This was the moment that Malcolm Simmons was transformed from an average, second string man to a Custom House star. He had given his side 14 points from a maximum of 15. To ice the cake, he went on to lead the field home in the scratch race final, again humbling Nygren and Luckhurst. It was even clearer that this was Simmons' golden night when it was noted that he had recorded the three fastest times

Malcolm Simmons and Peter Collins celebrate victory..

West Ham, 1966. From left to right: Ted Ede, Malcolm Simmons, Brian Leonard, Tom Price, Sevrre Harrfeldt, Norman Hunter, Reg Trott and Ken McKinlay on the bike.

of the evening. Anyone who saw the young Hammer that night would not have been surprised when he became one of England's leading riders from the late 1960s to the 1980s and runner-up in the 1976 World Championship.

After this drama, West Ham did not lose one official fixture for the remainder of the season. They made history by winning the treble: the Knockout Cup, the London Cup and, going to the last match against Cradley Heath, the first British League title. McKinlay and Harrfeldt completed the term with double figure averages. McKinlay's 10.72 put him in third place in the list of top League scorers – only Nigel Boocock and Barry Briggs could do better. Norman Hunter wasn't far behind Harrfeldt with 9.56. Simmons achieved a creditable 6.16 and Tony Clarke proved his potential with 5.16. The bells rang for the claret and blue.

Adding to team glory, Ken McKinlay was victorious in the Brandonapolis at Coventry, his former stamping ground. He also won the Silver Sash from Jim Lightfoot in May. McKinlay had defended the trophy with success on seven occasions, the longest unbeaten run for this title in 1965, when Bob Andrews took it from him in July. McKinlay also qualified for the World Championship final. He finished with just 4 points, but his thirteenth place was probably a confirmation of his exhaustion more than a reflection of his skill. Not to be totally outdone by his team-mate, Harrfeldt made the London Riders' Championship his at Hackney.

Competing in the newly formed British League, Ivan Mauger, for the first time, had a chance to ride against the best riders in the world. However, in his first official meeting of 1965 he broke an ankle (which from then on was held together by screws) and several foot bones. On crutches for most of the season, he came out to compete in the World Championship qualifying rounds wearing a reinforced boot and using a different riding style to cope. Remarkably, he qualified for the British Final at West Ham, although another fall at Wimbledon did not help his form, and the World Final passed him by that year. He did, however, go to Belle Vue for the British League Riders' Championship and notched up a creditable 8 points.

Dave Lanning and Phil Bishop took over the speedway management at Custom House in 1966. Terry Stone initially took Tony Clarke's place in the West Ham line-up, but later Don Smith, the famous trial rider, came into the side. The Custom House faithful had cause for optimism at the outset of the season, even though Sverre Harrfeldt was in Norway receiving treatment for a hernia. He would not return until West Ham were deep into their fixture list. The Hammers couldn't really get going at first, but things went from bad to worse in the summer. In June and July, West Ham contested eight matches: they lost seven, including three at Custom House. Holding on to the title was now a practical impossibility. However, the cockney boys won the final handful of their matches, saving some embarrassment by pushing themselves into seventh place. This, alongside the retention of the London Cup, made the season a respectable one. When Harrfeldt got back from Scandinavian convalescence, he put in some fine performances, but, like McKinlay, his form wasn't what it had been the previous year – although the pair did enough to remain club attractions. Hunter, Simmons, Leonard and Trott maintained approximately the same level of performance as they had in the preceding campaign, although Hunter won the London Riders' Championship and got third place in the British Riders' Championship.

Harrfeldt made it to World Championship in Gothenburg. The knowledgeable Swedish crowd was excited and entranced by his dynamic and expansive riding. Harrfeldt dropped just a single point, but despite a fantastic performance could not overcome the maximum point-taker, Barry Briggs, and had to be content with the runner-up spot. This was Briggs' fourth title. Ivan Mauger took fourth place in his maiden World Final, having regained full fitness. It was the culmination of an unprecedented run of success. He had finished as runner-up to Briggs in the British Final at Wimbledon and the Nordic-British Final at Sheffield. In his first appearance at Wembley, in the 1966 European Championship, after being beaten by Briggs in his first outing, he powered his way to victory in the next four rides to take his first major title.

Briggs, however, was still 'The Governor'. He had also become a master at the very demanding two-man Match Race events. In the Golden Helmet sponsored event, from 1963 until this contest was stopped at the end of 1966, Briggs dominated. He was unbeaten in the best of three races during 1965, and 1966. With the top league match scorers' Silver Sash Match Race event replacing the Golden Helmet, he again assumed the mantle of holder. With the backing of speedway's loyal supporters, Briggs had also moved speedway beyond the confines of its oval homesteads. In 1964 and in 1966, he was runner-up in the BBC TV *Sportsview* Sports Personality of the Year poll. On three occasions, he was highly placed in the equally all-embracing *Daily Express* competition.

The prestige value of these successes, not only to Barry but also to speedway in general, was a shock to those who were saying that speedway was dead.

Of Bikes And Men

Briggs won his 1966 World title on a JAWA bike. Up until this time, the machine had won a reputation as a tough bike able to smooth out bumpy East European circuits, but by his success on the world stage the New Zealand ace proved its suitability for British circuits.

The JAWA was a complete machine. It was factory-built, but unlike the JAP, which was just the engine, the frames were almost tailor-made for each individual rider. The JAWA was to grow in popularity with riders on the bigger tracks, because they seemed to have a little more 'top end' speed, whilst the JAP was more powerful in the lower ranges and therefore suitable for the smaller tracks. This is, of course, a very broad generalisation, for various engine tuners could alter the performances of either engine to suit the particular rider or track. But the bikes of this period, like their ancestors, were still stripped to the barest essentials. The tank held only enough alcohol fuel for two races and the seat was a thin, uncomfortable wedge of wood or metal.

West Ham's former master-tuner, Alex Moseley, died in 1966. He had been working as a consultant with an aircraft company. His tuning of speedway engines had become almost a hobby by that time and he served only about four riders, but their engines were the envy of all for their speed and reliability. Moseley had been the example that was to be followed by the tuners of the mid-to-late 1960s, many of whom were also riders. One such was the little Australian who performed his miracles at Hackney Wick, Jackie Biggs. He was one of the fastest workers that speedway had ever seen, and was quite often known to strip a clutch completely to pieces and rebuild it in between races at a meeting, a job which normally took two or three hours.

Return Of The Tests

Test matches were resumed in 1966. Australia had caught the backlash of the formation of the British League and interest in speedway had markedly improved in all major Australian cities. The young Australian rider was again prepared to give the sport a fling, knowing that if he displayed talent he would be virtually assured of a place in British League racing. New Zealand had also become something of a British nursery – Barry Briggs, Ronnie Moore and Ivan Mauger having really put New Zealand on the speedway map. These three giants were the backbone of the New Zealand international squad. As they held British racing licences, they were also permitted to represent Great Britain.

In this year, Ray Wilson pitted himself against the best riders in the country, competing in every League match and topping the Archers' averages, at 8.60 per match. An invitation to race in Australia was accepted that winter, and the season at Adelaide's Rowley Park helped to broaden his experience. He rode for England against Scotland three times in 1966.

11
DECLINE AND FALL

The Colour Marshal

As his title indicates, the Colour Marshal is the man responsible for seeing that every rider has the correct colour cover on his helmet. Whilst most of the time this may seem very simple, and in fact it is, there are occasions when his job can be a nightmare. Consider a position when the helmet colours at his disposal are all in the possession of the riders who will need them for their future races. Suddenly there is an accident and a rider is carried off in an ambulance complete with all his equipment including his helmet cover. A reserve is going to take his place and needs a helmet cover. Now the Colour Marshal must chase up one that he has previously issued to another rider, but he does not want to take one from a rider who might be appearing in the very next race, so he looks for one whose heat is not so close. Think however, of the time when such a rider is temporarily missing, perhaps attending to something on his machine away from the main section of the pits. While the Marshal is searching for him, the Clerk of the Course is bursting a blood vessel, suddenly the team manager realises that instead of a reserve he can use some other rider. He cannot tell the Colour Marshal because he is missing owing to his search … you can imagine the temporary chaos! So the Colour Marshal needs to be a methodical type who can keep control in all situations.

Silver, L. 'The Vital Cogs' in *The Speedway Annual* compiled by Silver, L. and Douglas, P. (London, Pelham Books, 1969)

Reg Trott and Don Smith were replaced when Tony Clarke and Stan Stevens returned to Custom House in 1967. The three heat-leaders started the season in fine form and this, alongside a good team effort from the rest of the side, meant that West Ham were able to impress in the first weeks of the new term. On 13 June, the Hammers took the substantial scalp of Wimbledon and moved to top place in the League. Two weeks later, West Ham had experienced defeat only once in a dozen matches of League contest. However, on 30 June the run ended in a local derby with Hackney at Custom House. To rub it in, on American Independence Day the boys from the Wick bea West Ham down on the marshes. In August, the Hammers were still the League leaders, but this double blow by their cockney rivals seemed to have hit the side's morale hard and they were unable to maintain championship form. West Ham had fallen to the number three spot when the season concluded, although only three points separated the Custom

House crew from the victorious Swindon. The end of the season marked the departure of Malcolm Simmons, creating the space that was to be filled by George Barclay in 1968.

West Ham made the final of the Knockout Cup, but found Coventry too good for them on the day, going down 104-88 to the Midlanders. It might have been different if injury hadn't kept Sverre Harrfeldt out of the home leg, but the Hammers held on to the London Cup for the third consecutive year. They got some retribution from defeating the Hounds of Hackney and then went on to beat Wimbledon, both home and away. Harrfeldt rode in three cup matches, scoring maximum points in each contest. He had made 13 maximums in League competition and had the best average, 10.44. McKinlay got a creditable 8 maximums, 6 of them paid, with an average of 9.46. Hunter's average, on the other hand, fell to 7.57, just marginally better than Simmons. Stan Stevens recorded 4.46. The disparity in the total of paid maximums represented the gap that separated McKinlay's and Harrfeldt's attitude to team work. Club skipper McKinlay was like Norman Parker and Ronnie Moore of Wimbledon, in that he would consistently keep an eye out for his partner going into the initial bend. If his 'oppo' was with him, he would let him move up and then attempt to block the opposition.

Ray Wilson's average for the British League rose to a creditable 10.36 per match (out of a possible 12). He was beginning to hit the headlines on a national scale. He qualified for the British Final at West Ham, where his 10-point tally took him to his World Final debut and his first ride at Wembley Stadium. Showing no trace of big night nerves, he won his initial race, the opening heat of the meeting, and continued to ride well. The World Championship final was devoid of claret and blue, but one-time Custom House man Bengt Jansson was runner-up following a run-off against Ove Fundin, who had been tempted out of retirement and away from his flourishing haulage business to ride five times at Long Eaton. This was the last of his record five Championship wins. He had only finished out of the first three places once in twelve years and the reason for his single absence in 1966 was his suspension by the Swedish authorities for competing in a car-race meeting when he was due to ride in a World Championship qualifying round. Between 1954 and the end of the 1960s, he only missed the 1966 Final.

Ivan Mauger made third place in the World Final, being the top British entry. He was now an automatic selection for every Great Britain international team. In the West Ham qualifier, Ray Wilson finished in a creditable eighth place, adding to his win in the all-star Tadeusz Teodorowicz Memorial Trophy at Swindon and the Laurels at Wimbledon, both after run-offs. Wilson had also made second place behind Barry Briggs in the Scottish Open Championship and the Pride of the Midlands event. Last but not least, he was third in both the British League Riders' Championship and the Midland Riders' Championship. He rode for Great Britain against Sweden and Poland in the Tests and was then selected for the World Team Cup squad to compete in the final at Mälmo in Sweden. Wilson was also to ride for England during the tour of Australia, where the visitors won the series 3-2.

The prevailing harmony in the ranks of British speedway gave the sport a chance to expand in 1968. Initial work to create a second division was not successful, but eventually the British League was able to encompass ten new tracks and produce another division. The season began on 2 April and Wimbledon were the visitors to a snow-covered Custom House – one of the Dons, former Hammer Reg Luckhurst, asked a photographer to take a picture so that he could use it for his Christmas cards!

With the departure of Malcolm Simmons at the end of the previous season, the West Ham side found it hard to achieve equilibrium; the Hammers had a gap between the established heat-leader threesome and the second-rowers. For all that, the team were holding their own until, in the European Final, top Hammer Harrfeldt was involved in a serious smash that was to put him out of action for the rest of the season. Harrfeldt was a beautiful rider and a good-looking man, hence his nickname 'Heartthrob'. His balance and power was complimented by a flamboyant style. His sprints along the fence at Custom House hardly ever failed to bring the stadium to its feet. Up until his crash, Harrfeldt had been dogged by mechanical problems and sluggish starts. This induced him to produce even more spectacular displays when he did get into his rides. Few who saw the Norwegian will forget how he would hunt down the man at the front. He had a brave riding style that involved added risks of the type of crash that he suffered in the European Final, where his leg and pelvis were broken.

Injury also claimed McKinlay and Hunter, but West Ham managed to hold on and ended up in sixth place. Harrfeldt, Hunter and McKinlay each finished with averages over 9. Brian Leonard totalled 5.36 and the reliable Stan Stevens again notched up 4.46. Ronnie Moore won the New Zealand Championship in 1968 and this motivated British promoters Len Silver and Ronnie Greene to entice Ronnie to return to British racing. Eventually, Greene made an offer of a two-year contract that couldn't be refused and Moore opened the season with Wimbledon, the start of a six-year stint with the Dons. Following a slow start, Moore, mounted on a JAP machine, was soon knocking out double-figure scores home and away. He won the Wimbledon World Championship qualifying round against the reigning world title holder and the British Champion of that year, Ivan Mauger. He also beat England stars Terry Betts, Tony Clarke, Reg Luckhurst and Trevor Hedge, this demonstrated that Moore was again able to challenge the elite.

Ivan Mauger, who had scored consistently in League speedway that season, found himself in dispute with the Newcastle management. He asked for a transfer and Belle Vue was not slow to come in for him. He produced a devastating performance in the World Championships, winning two qualifying rounds, a semi-final and then, with an unbeaten score chart, he went on to win, in succession, the British Final, the European semi-final and, with 10 points at the European Final in Wroclaw in Poland, he topped the British entries for the World Final at Gothenburg. In the World Final, he was again in scintillating form, winning all of his five rides with consummate ease to become only the fourth man to win the title with maximum points (the others were Tommy Price in 1949, Ronnie Moore in 1954 and 1959, and Barry Briggs in 1958, 1964 and 1966). Mauger's three-point advantage over the second-placed Barry Briggs was the greatest title victory margin since the series had started in 1936. Jancarz of Poland took third place.

This result very much reflected the future of the sport: New Zealand domination alongside expansion in Eastern Europe. Mona Fundin, who was always an ardent follower of speedway, was at the 1968 World Final acting as a reporter for her local newspaper. Her husband, Ove, had ridden in Britain that year, turning out 12 times in League matches for Belle Vue (whose Swedish star Soren Sjosten had broken a leg). A broken foot picked up a month prior to the final riding for New Zealand against England at Newcastle limited Ronnie Moore's performance.

Moore was able to achieve some consolation for his disappointing form in Sweden. His Wimbledon side won the British League Knockout Cup for the second time. In 1969 ,he was again to lead the Dons as their skipper in the expanded British League, which at this time included thirty-five teams.

Following his return home to New Zealand for the first time since 1963 at the end of the 1968 season, racing in Los Angeles and Australia on the way, Ivan Mauger entered 1969 thinking faster than most. He alternated between JAP and JAWA machines, realising that there were tracks more suited to one than the other. His staggering 11-point plus average in British League encounters pinpoints his logic.

At West Ham it was clear that Sverre Harrfeldt would be unable to compete that season, such were the extent of his injuries. West Ham found a commensurate replacement, signing Wimbledon's Olle Nygren, but the Hammers still had problems. Norman Hunter had moved on and there was no one to fill his place as heat-leader. Norwegian Bernt Norregard was brought in, as was Australian John Langfield, but both failed to impress. In desperation, the Hammers looked for someone from the existing team roster to plug the gap left by Harrfeld. Tony Clarke was the man to be given the responsibility and he took up the challenge well. It seemed to motivate him to be third heat-leader and he pelted to the top of the averages and took the mantle of number one Hammer.

However, Harrfeldt and Hunter were sorely missed, and with McKinlay's average falling to a disappointing 7.69, West Ham found themselves second from bottom of the League at the end of the term. It was the worst season that Custom House had experienced since the start of the British League. Adding to the misery was the fact that the Hammers had been eliminated from the Knockout Cup in the first round, having been overcome by Kings Lynn following two tied matches.

A third place in the British Final qualified Ronnie Moore for his thirteenth World Championship appearance. The Final came at the end of a season in which Barry Briggs had been plagued by injury. A fall during the Test match with Sweden at Wolverhampton (where Nigel Boocock also broke his collarbone) saw Barry sustain a badly torn and broken right thumb. Medical advice urged at least two months in splints and plaster, with no riding – otherwise Briggs would run the risk of permanently losing the use of his thumb. In typical fashion, 'Briggo' tore off the plaster to qualify for the World Final, via semi-final, British Final, Nordic-British and European Finals. His thumb was a problem in Gothenburg, and Briggs became feverish on the night of the European Final. Not wanting to waver, he wrapped himself in blankets between races.

Although Ken McKinlay had experienced a very poor year, he also reached the World Championship Final – something he had not managed since 1965. A wonderful victory over Ove Fundin in his third ride put him in with a chance of getting into the first three

Ivan Mauger – World Champion at Reading on 19 April 1971.

– and a chance of victory – going into his last two rides with 7 points. Regrettably, the penultimate and final races brought him not a single point. He left Wembley in eighth place. Ivan Mauger and Barry Briggs finished in the same order as 1968. The Swedish Hammer Sjosten got on the tractor with them. In the same year, partnered by Bob Andrews, Mauger also took the World Best Pairs title.

Briggs was eventually diagnosed as having contracted septicaemia, and fears were expressed for his affected leg and even his life. For all this, Briggs had his mind on the one trophy that had eluded him: the World Team Cup. He virtually got out of his sick bed to captain Great Britain in this event. His riding example inspired a team spirit and pride hitherto lacking in the British efforts to win the competition. With Ivan Mauger scoring maximum points, Briggs led his side to victory and a place in speedway history.

It was not until the latter part of the season that Ray Wilson hit the type of form he had been known for over the previous few seasons. Maybe he was suffering from a hint of staleness after almost three years of non-stop racing at home and abroad. But he timed his return to winning ways well, to take the East Midlands Open and the cheque for £100. He represented England in the Best Pairs competition in Norway, and rode in the Czechoslovakian Golden Helmet meetings, as well as competing in home internationals. However, for once he wasn't his team's top scorer, being pipped at the post by Swede Anders Michenek for the honour of representing his team at Belle Vue's annual British League Riders' Cup final.

The Eastern European expansion continued. It was also around this time that Czech riders started to join the Poles, who had begun moving to Britain and appearing for British League clubs in much the same way as the Swedes, Danish and Norwegians had ten years previously. Official figures showed that speedway overtook soccer as Poland's number one spectator sport in 1969. Further south, Brazil was looking as if it would take over from Venezuela and Argentina as speedway's leading country in Latin America. It was in 1969 that Brazil asked Britain's SCB for advice on how to run the sport.

Three young riders began to show potential at the end of the 1960s. As the 1969 season reached its final few matches, Barry Crowson was gaining regular selection for the West Ham side, as was Martyn Piddock. The sixteen-year-old Dave Jessup had three outings – he was just 5ft 5in tall but was to have a big future in speedway. Jessup was born in Suffolk and made his name through the Kent Youth Motorcycle Club grass-track events. He became club champion at fifteen, but on his sixteenth birthday he joined Eastbourne in British League Division Two. He was then the youngest rider in speedway. He spent a season with the Eagles, before joining West Ham for a short period, going on to sign for the revitalised Wembley Lions.

In the late 1960s, Leicester skipper Ray Wilson was speedway's answer to soccer's George Best. In his early twenties, he was a dark-haired, handsome, well-built, muscular young man and he was the idol of the Midland tracks. With something of the stand-up and blast-it style of his great idol, Barry Briggs, Ray's gating was good, but he was not always at his best coming from behind. Surprisingly, he turned in some of his best performances when the track was wet – not a favourite condition with the majority of riders.

However, if the world of speedway belonged to anyone in late 1960s, it was Barry Briggs. In 1968, the Wimbledon track record detailed in each week's programme still showed Barry Brigg's time made in 1955. The only man to beat him in 1968 was Ivan Mauger, the rider who had forced Briggs into second place in two World Championships. He had, at various times, ridden with arm or leg or foot heavily strapped up and padded, showing his dedication, determination and fighting spirit. He knew that every week out of the saddle in mid-season was one week's less competitive experience. He once said: 'You can't afford to lose that knife-edge slickness of eyes, reflexes and brain co-ordination, and hope to come back and be with them again right away.'

The British Championship initiated in 1961 had, by 1969, been won by Briggs on six occasions; the other three times he had been runner-up. He had won the British League Riders' Championship final every year since its inception in 1965. He had been all-star Internationale winner, taken the London Riders' Championship, the Midland Riders' Championship, the Pride of the South, Pride of the Midlands and the Brandonapolis. Briggs had been the Champion of New Zealand, taken the Welsh Open, The Laurels, The Olympique, been Champion of Champions and Scottish Open

Champion. He had four World Championship titles under his belt – an event he had competed in a record-shattering sixteen consecutive times, never finishing lower than sixth since his first appearance in 1954. In 1969, he was in his thirty-fifth year, with seventeen seasons to his credit. During this time, 'Bee-Bee' had ridden for Wimbledon, New Cross, Southampton and, from 1965, Swindon. He had made 94 international appearances: 19 for New Zealand, 30 for Australasia, and 45 for Great Britain.

West Ham's Women

The 1970 season of the British League opened with thirty-six teams involved. West Ham's fan base continued to hold up well. Speedway always had had a relatively large number of female fans, particularly when compared to, for example, football, but West Ham Speedway seemed to have a particular attraction for woman supporters. It is hard to say why this should be. Maybe it has something to do with the lack of violence or trouble at speedway meetings, although the supporters were not angels. Perhaps there was the appeal of speed and/or the presence of many good-looking men, including fine examples of Australian, New Zealand or Canadian manhood. Whatever the reasons, it was not unusual for families to have generations of women involved in support. Woman fans of the 1960s would have been told about the old riders and the history of the club by their mothers and grandmothers, many of these women having been ardent supporters in the pre- and post-war periods. This maternal line would also tell young women, long before they were able to attend matches themselves, about the fun to be had at meetings and on coach trips away from Custom House.

Women supporting West Ham was thus a part of East London culture and tradition, and a female rite of passage in the area. Many young women starting to attend in the 1960s thought they knew what to expect, but they often found that it was much better than they could have imagined. The crowd at West Ham was a fraternity that shared the joy of victory and sadness when losing. For a whole group of East End women, speedway became part of their lives and a way of life. They spent their hard-earned wages on hats and scarves, badges, mascots, teddies, autograph books, programmes and glossy pictures of favourite riders. Speedway was something akin to pop music in its appeal to young women, but this was a much more multi-faceted passion. Unless you have actually been a speedway fan, the involvement is hard to understand. There's the kick of the races, the smell, the noise, the pulse of excitement from the spectators. West Ham meetings, with their big crowds, were particularly vibrant. The Hammers' women supporters were amongst the noisiest at times, especially at away games. They would make their presence felt, both in the grounds and when walking to them, shouting and singing their favourite chants:

> *Zigger Zagger, Zigger Zagger, Oi Oi Oi!*
> *Zigger Zagger, Zigger Zagger, Oi Oi Oi!*
> *One for, two for, who the hell are we for,*
> *WEST HAM, WEST HAM!*

Autograph-hunting was something of an obsession with most of the teenage women fans. They would hang about in places where riders might loiter or pass by. It was something of a competition as to who could get the greatest number of autographs, or the rarest examples. Ivan Mauger was probably the most difficult to find, and many young women desperately wanted his signature. It was Mauger's habit to rush away once meetings had concluded, but youthful female fans would go to great lengths to procure his signature, including coach trips to the home of Mauger's team, Belle Vue, Manchester. It was not unusual to see them walking away from him, star-struck, smiling from ear to ear with their books closed protecting their most precious moniker.

A West Ham favourite at the time was Martyn Piddock. Many young women would have numerous copies of his autograph, getting examples week after week. It didn't seem to matter how many times they had it, they would just get on the end of the queue and get it again. There are many attics of former 'West Ham Women' filled with autograph books – the product of endless patience, devotion and endeavour. They are often held on to because they represent days full of happiness, invariably remembered with great affection.

Lokeren Tears

Perhaps the worst day in speedway history dawned on Tuesday 14 July 1970. Little known today outside speedway circles, it was certainly the most tragic event in the sporting annals of the East End of London and West Ham speedway in particular. A minibus carrying the West Ham team back from a match in Holland, heading for Ostend, crashed into two lorries, a petrol tanker and then into the side of a farmhouse near the small town of Lokeren in Belgium. The bus was split in two. Malcolm Carmichael and Martyn Piddock were killed instantly. Peter Bradshaw and Gary Everett (who had ridden for Wimbledon) were also killed, as was West Ham's legendary team manager, the former King of Crash, Phil Bishop, who died in hospital. Bishop, in his riding days, had been known as the India rubber man; he had broken every bone in his body and been able to bounce back. Stan Stevens and Colin Pratt were seriously injured but later recovered, although Pratt never rode again. Mechanic Roy Sullivan suffered a broken leg and another rider, Garry Hay, had severe cuts to his head and face. The Dutch bus driver, who had fallen asleep at the wheel, also died.

The news of the crash devastated the fans and the area in general. At West Ham Stadium, the flags were flown at half-mast and the first meeting after the accident was a very moving experience. The crowd were silent and numb. Before the meeting started, a lone trumpet played the Last Post. Supporters were moved to tears. It was like one huge family sharing its grief. It is a moment that anyone attending that night will never forget. John McNulty, the manager of the Speedway Control Board, said: 'This terrible accident is to speedway what the Manchester United air disaster was to football.'

The Lokeren disaster darkened West Ham's year. However, even before the calamity, the side had profound problems. McKinlay, Stevens and Langfield had gone. Harrfeldt was back but his confidence had been lost and he broke his arm on 12 May, putting him out of action yet again. New signing Antonin Kasper from Czechoslovakia was anonymous in the first weeks of the season, when Leonard and Crowson also decided to leave. Finally, promoter Dave Lanning left what was increasingly looking like a sinking ship. The former Norwich promoter, Gordon Parkins took over as promoter/speedway manager.

Clarke and Nygren began well enough but, for no apparent reason, Clarke lost his form and only found it again at the end of the season. Stevens did come back after a while, but at the time the Lokeren tragedy occurred, only Nygren kept the team ticking over – although some support was starting to come from new signing, young Swede Christer Lofqvist. Lofqvist was reminiscent of Harrfeldt, a round-the-boards expert and an exciting rider. By degrees, the scores got better and, by the end of the season, Lofqvist had established himself as second only to Nygren. Following the death of Phil Bishop at Lokeren, Sverre Harrfeldt took over as team manager, and would later on make a comeback to the team as reserve.

The season's end saw Nygren on an average of 9.33. Lofqvist had scored 7.59 and Clarke, 7.51. In eleven matches, Harrfeldt had managed no more than 4.85. West Ham were again confined to penultimate position in the table. With Belle Vue dismissing them from the Knockout Cup in the first round, 1970 had been a bad year.

12

THE FINAL HAMMER

The Speedway Manager

Most often this man is not one of the usual track staff; he is usually the promoter, for he is directly responsible to the referee and the Speedway Control Board for the complete running and organisation of the meeting, including seeing that it runs to time. He could be termed a 'co-ordinator' for that is really his job, to ascertain that all the officials and riders are properly equipped and ready to run. He is the man who takes the final responsibility for all the decisions, excepting those by the referee of course, and he may have to make up his mind in a split second over a particular course of action. For example, the meeting is running late due to perhaps an accident, should he shorten the interval, or should he cut out a race in the second half of the programme? Above all he is a man who has to make decisions, and woe betide him if he makes a wrong one! Silver, L. 'Anatomy of a Speedway' in *The Speedway Annual* compiled by Silver, L. and Douglas, P. (London, Pelham Books, 1969)

The British League's policy of cautious advancement seemed to have given the sport a firm foundation, while the BSPA had proved a constant source of new ideas for expansion. More areas were being probed for possible centres, and plans advanced for a third division to operate in 1971. Speedway has been called a family sport, and it seemed to have captured the imaginations of enough households in the late 1960s to make the catastrophic days of the 1950s no more than a bad memory.

The sport also continued its global expansion, gaining a foothold in the east, where Japan – very much a law unto itself in the speedway world – was the only country that allowed betting on speedway events. Jimmy Ogisu became the first Japanese rider to appear in Britain when he took part in a few meetings in 1970. There were also reports that Chinese observers had watched speedway meetings in the USSR. South Africa had shown some interest in speedway in the 1950s, but for some time little was heard of the sport in the African continent, until late in 1970, when it was introduced in what was then Rhodesia, where speedway got under way at Salisbury, Bulawayo, and Gwelo.

Although Gothenburg was to stage the event in 1971, the USSR were pressing for the right to organise the World Final. However, strong Polish claims for recognition in the world of speedway were answered in September 1970, when a capacity crowd of 65,000 watched the World Championship final in Wroclaw. Ivan Mauger became the first man to win the title three years in a row (for the second time with maximum points) – a performance all the more creditable in view of the fact that his two previous wins were at Gothenburg and Wembley. At the age of thirty-one, he proved his mastery of all types of tracks.

Although Barry Briggs missed the 1971 World Final he had triumphed four times in his 17 appearances in World Championship finals up to 1970. Most winners at that point had come from New Zealand, Sweden, and, in the early years, Australia. England had produced only two winners, Tommy Price and Peter Craven (twice).

By 1971, the JAWA was probably a more popular machine in Britain than the JAP. Speedway motorcycles were powered by 500cc engines, except for those taking part in domestic British meetings, which allowed a maximum 510cc. Before the race they were bump-started, then held on the clutch until the race began (in earlier days of the sport, some narrow tracks, such as Stamford Bridge, allowed rolling starts). Frames and handle-bars had changed over the years, largely because of the drastic alterations in cornering technique that modern riders pioneered. Early machines had low-slung handlebars and long frames suitable for the spectacular trailing-leg technique. This involved the rider broadsiding round the bends with his left (or nearside) leg trailing behind and his knee almost touching the track. As a spectacle this style has no equal, but it was ousted by the more efficient foot-forward technique, which involved the rider sitting in a much more upright position on a machine with upswept handlebars and short frames.

Although it was difficult to improve on the modern sophisticated machinery, many riders did make minor modifications to their machines to suit their own style. The limited nature of the speedway market deterred manufacturers from producing new speedway machines, but there was some hope as the 1970s moved on that America or Japan might come up with something new if speedway caught on in a big way in one or both of these countries.

As Wimbledon's number one for the year, former Hammer Dave Jessup qualified for the big Division Two meeting of the year, the Riders' Championship, at Hackney's Waterden Road. Jessup's entry defied a Speedway Control Board ban: the SCB had thought he was too good to be entered and should be considered a full-time Division One rider. After a day of argument, Dave was allowed to compete. He won convincingly, beating Barry Crowson and Gary Peterson in the process. Jessup went to the tapes for his last race with four wins under his belt. Although out-gated in his last ride, Jessup kept calm and collected two points for second place. This was enough to give him the distinction of becoming the youngest ever champion. The teenage Jessup was to become an estab-lished Young England rider, turning out against the Czechs, Swedes and Australasians in 1970.

Goodbye To Love … There Are No Tomorrows

In the FIM Internationale held at Wimbledon in 1971, Ronnie Moore had four wins from his first four rides and needed just a second place in his last race to take the champi-onship for the first time. However, during his final ride while leading Ivan Mauger and Ole

Great Britain v. Rest of the World in 1972 – an incredibly strong side. From left to right, back row: Eric Boocock, Ray Wilson, Reg Fearman (manager), Reg Luckhurst and Trevor Hedge. Front row: Nigel Boocock, Ronnie Moore, Barry Briggs and Ivan Mauger.

Olsen, his JAP slipped from underneath him on the last bend of the third lap and his chance of winning was gone.

Moore was to turn out for his fourteenth World Final in September. Only two riders, Ove Fundin on fifteen appearances and Barry Briggs on eighteen, were to make more showings. But Ronnie was again let down by his JAP, his meagre 5 points and eleventh place demonstrating that it could not compete against the faster JAWA machines, and this led him to retire from international speedway. It was time to think of the future and he opened a motorbike shop with another New Zealand rider, Graeme Stapleton, but he still could not give up the game completely, riding in New Zealand and Britain for the first World League series and for the Ivan Mauger/Barry Briggs World Superstars Inc. – a nomadic troupe of World Champions, roaming the world.

The British League continued to maintain thirty-six teams in 1971, but West Ham were not one of the best; in fact, at Custom House things went from bad to worse. A new team manager was appointed in the shape of former Hammer, Howdy Byford, but this could not compensate for the fact that the decision had been made to sell the stadium for redevelopment.

Clarke and Harrfeldt moved to Wembley, whilst Kasper failed to make another appearance for the Hammers. Reg Luckhurst was back and some new blood came into the West Ham side, including Preben Rosenkilde, Mick Handley, Alan Belham and Alan Sage. As the season wore on, Stan Stevens made a number of Custom House appearances, but was to move on to Romford before the fixture list was completed. Handley was exchanged for Barry Duke, but it didn't seem to matter what formation West Ham attempted, the results just wouldn't go their way. For all that, Lofqvist had a decent year. Continuing to threaten the safety fence during every ride, he gave some awesome exhibitions of speedway craft, rescuing his team from what would otherwise have been a series of embarrassing defeats. Nygren's performance deteriorated at the same time as third heat-leader Luckhurst seemed to be losing his touch, averaging just 6.51.

At the start of May, the Hammers went down badly to Halifax – a side that was to finish in fifteenth place in the League – in the first round of the Speedway Star Cup, 29-49. As it turned out, this was to be the shape of things to come.

From the company chairman, Eric Cargill, down to the track staff (who were appointed on an unpaid basis during West Ham's final season, such was the promotion's financial plight), there came the frequent complaint that the British League authorities were complicit in the demise of the club. It was regularly alleged that they were not prepared to afford West Ham the sort of assistance that would have been forthcoming to any other team still reeling from a disaster of the type West Ham had been hit by in Lokren. However, perhaps predictably, the British League powers always strenuously denied this. Throughout that final season, West Ham occupied bottom place in the table, from which at no time did they look like escaping. There was visible discord among members of the team that wore the traditional red and blue halves and white crossed hammers and, at one stage, Cargill made public his fears that, 'we might not even see the season out'. For West Ham, it was an uncharacteristically dismal response set against such a pulsating past.

West Ham finished at the foot of the League table and withdrew from the British League Division One. The dust had hardly settled when the fatal message came:

The board of directors of West Ham Speedway Ltd. very much regret to announce that they have been informed by West Ham Stadium Ltd. (a subsidiary of GRA Property Trust Ltd.) – owners of the West Ham Stadium site – that no guarantee can be given that the stadium will be available for a full season in the First Division of the British Speedway League in 1972.

It was not a sudden execution, but a long-awaited formal moment of reckoning that sooner or later would have caught up with West Ham. The arena, once East London's answer to Wembley Stadium, had become a huge white elephant. Soon afterwards the grey stone walls, green corrugated stands and dated bench seats that were now showing their age were sold, and the racing licence went to the thriving young Ipswich side. Between July 1928 and October 1971 – the war years and the eight-year spell covering the period 1955 to 1962 excepted – West Ham were an essential part of British speedway. This had been a team whose followers had sampled just about every emotion and every spectacle any sport could provide. The side was always groundbreaking. West Ham was the first tack to boast a silver sand racing surface. Under lights this gave speedway a totally new visual dimension. Fifty years previously, West Ham's management were the first to go out and buy themselves a reigning world champion, Jack Young, in the transfer market. It was West Ham who set the pace upon launching the British League in 1965, when they were inaugural champions.

In December, the owners of Custom House stadium, the Greyhound Racing Association (GRA), who had taken over the stadium in 1967, made it known that the arena had been sold to a property developer for £475,000. There had never been much hope of rejuvenating the stadium, or developing a new speedway venue on the site. The land that the arena was built on had always been prone to subsidence and the lumbering old amphitheatre was never well connected in terms of public transport. Furthermore, noise pollution in what was an urbanised area was always going to be a problem. There was some speculation that a new stadium would be built in the Docklands, giving the Hammers a new home, but that never got off the ground. It began to look as though it was the end for West Ham speedway.

New York, Europe, The World

Barry Briggs was instrumental in bringing speedway to the Middle East and 'repopularising' the sport on the other side of the Atlantic. In the winter that bridged the gap between the 1968 and 1969 seasons, he twice went to the USA to compete on speedway and at indoor concrete-bowl events, trying to make his dream of opening American eyes to speedway come true. He brought the sport to New York's Madison Square Garden in 1971; a huge crowd cheered as Briggs, the New Zealand 'villain' of the night, fell. The meeting's success encouraged hopes of an American speedway revival. Speedway continued its European expansion with most continental countries having staged the sport by the start of the 1970s. From humble pre-war beginnings, Scandinavian riders had, for some time, been able to challenge the British and Commonwealth for domination of speedway. By 1971, Sweden had won the World Team Cup six times since its inauguration in 1960, compared with one solitary success by Great Britain. Ove Fundin, who with five victories had the best record of any rider in the World Championships up to 1971, was Sweden's standard-bearer. Norway, with riders such as former Hammer Sverre Harrfeldt and Reidar Eide, and Denmark, with Ole Olsen, helped widen speedway's international horizons.

Olsen, who won the World Championship for the first time in September 1971 signalled a period of dominance by Denmark. He probably lacked a little in consistency, but on his day he was arguably the greatest rider of them all and certainly the best rider to ever come out of Denmark. He was the first Dane to win a world motor sport title and, in the same year as he won the world title, he took the Danish, Nordic and New South Wales titles plus the Danish 1,000-metre Sand-Track Championship. It was quite a remarkable record for a twenty-four-year-old, and he crowned his achievements by being elected Denmark's Sportsman of the Year.

Finland too was beginning to show considerable interest in the sport. However, speedway's biggest success story up to the start of the 1970s was probably its development in Poland, Eastern Europe's leading speedway nation at the time and four-times winner of the World Team Cup. But the USSR was catching up. Igor Plechanov, their 1971 chief trainer, twice finished as runner-up in a World Championship final. By the start of the 1970s, most experts rated the USSR fourth strongest of the speedway nations behind Britain and the Commonwealth, Sweden and Poland. However, the Soviets were already being strongly challenged by Czechoslovakia, a country that produced some good international riders, despite a dearth of local speedway meetings.

Bombers Over The Docks

Wally Mawdsley and Pete Lansdale had been obliged to close Romford Speedway's Brookland Stadium after a history of complaints about noise from local residents. They negotiated one more speedway season at Custom House with the property developers, who were to bulldoze the former Hammers stadium. The stay of execution would last until October 1972. So, annexing the former Romford nickname (they had sported an RAF roundel on their race jackets), Second Division West Ham Bombers were incarnated at Custom House. Stan Stevens was signed to skipper the side that included Brian Foote, Kevin Holden, Bob Coles, Ted Howgego, Mike Sampson, Charlie Benham, Mike Lanham, Vic Cross and Jan Gills.

However, as May began, the developers changed their minds and announced their intention to close the stadium by the end of the month. As such, after a handful of matches, the Bombers disappeared into history. Mawdsley and Lansdale transferred their license and moved the Holker Street side to Barrow. On 23 May, the final speedway meeting took place at Custom House. West Ham rode against Hull. The Bombers were narrowly beaten 38-40. Top scorers for West Ham were Stan Stevens and Mike Lanham, gaining 9 apiece. Stevens might have done better, but suffered with engine problems in his first race. Tony Childs of Hull won the last-ever League race at the Custom House Stadium.

As the night drew in for a great speedway track, so the end of a great speedway rider's career drew to a close. Ronnie Moore's last full-time season in England was 1972. Again he topped the Wimbledon points averages, but elimination at the British Final stage of the World Championship was a disappointment, albeit that Ronnie was on a spare bike as a result of his usual machine having recently been wrecked in a crash with Nigel Boocock. However, Ronnie's British career finished on a high note

Ole Olsen – Danish Claret and Blue.

143

with third place in the British League Riders' Championship and a win in the London Riders' Championship, some twenty years on from the first time he had lifted the trophy.

Ronnie Moore was married to Jill Turner, a showgirl with the famous Windmill Theatre. This is perhaps fitting as Moore was, by way of his ability and daring, a speedway showman. He was the complete speedway rider: a natural, a superb stylist. His was the era in which speedway skill was more important than sheer speed. In those golden days, bike development was not so important as the riders' talent. Moore epitomised this. He rode with intelligence, using his brain all the time, and there was never a smarter rider.

Barry Briggs was persuaded to lead his former club, Wimbledon, and although a long way from the all-conquering 'Briggo' of old, he still maintained a healthy 9-point British League average. On the international scene he looked set, in the twilight of his career, to equal Ove Fundin's five World titles at Wembley in 1972. After impressively winning his first ride, he was dismounted by two rampaging Russians in his second outing, losing the index finger of his left hand in one of the most dramatic crashes ever witnessed in a World Final.

Briggs always knew what it meant being 'top gun' in the sport. He once said: 'Every time I go up to the line, I know that the other riders are going to try and pull out that extra something, and beat me.' But there are limits to how much anybody can take and the sign of a true champion and professional is knowing when to step down. That injury caused Barry to ponder his future for, having literally won everything the sport had to offer, the time seemed right to retire and it was no surprise when, in a TV interview, he announced the end of his racing days.

Briggs was able to race and ride motorcycles in any environment with almost equal expertise. He competed successfully on grass-tracks and Continental long-track events, on shale, road, scrambles, trials, ice and even on crushed anthills in Kenya. It is true that he probably would not beat top road racers like Surtees, Hallwood, Agostini, Sheene and Read, or scrambles stars like John Banks, Vic Eastwood and Dave Bickers in their respective fields, but he would have given any of them a run for their money on their own turf. He has been universally recognised by World Champions at all the differing forms of two-wheeled sport as the best all-rounder. 'I cannot live with him at speedway', said one famous world road champion, 'But give him an hour to practise at Brands Hatch and I will have difficulty shaking him off at my sport.'

Within the speedway discipline, Briggs thrilled fans with his own brand of aggressive muscular racing. He treated tracks of all shapes and sizes with equal ability, the stand-up, full-throttle style riding of 'Briggo' was a sight to thrill the eye of all who appreciate the finesse of such a technique that ensures rear-wheel drive at all times. His ability to come from behind was matched by no one. This fact made Briggs, in front or behind, the most dangerous and most difficult rider to beat.

Briggs was, in fact, an all-round sports enthusiast. He played soccer for the Speedway Riders' XI, enjoyed golf and swimming, and was a Southampton and Chelsea supporter. He served all his clubs – Wimbledon, New Cross, Southampton and, for nearly ten seasons when he never failed to record less than a 10-point average, the Swindon Robins – with commitment and professional focus. Barry's wife, June, met Briggs when she was a Wimbledon supporter, making the pilgrimage to Plough Lane every week. She showed how much she realised the extent to which speedway was a part of him when she said: 'I always worry for Barry. But speedway is part of him. Take that away and he isn't the same man. Without speedway, I would never have met him. I would never have fallen in love with him. We would never have married.'

At Custom House on Tuesday 13 June 1972, ironically, the weather was not too bad after several years when it always seemed to rain on Tuesdays – speedway day at Custom House. There was no speedway at West Ham on that Tuesday. There were no riders there either. There were some stadium officials, an auctioneer and some businessmen looking for a bargain or two among the fixtures and fittings that went under the hammer that day.

No one wanted a safety fence or the starting gate. The Hammers had played just about every audience possible, from Royalty to the under-privileged East End kids. Millions had passed through its turnstiles and gates. They all enjoyed the time they had spent in the old edifice, but after the last bid was made and buyers and sellers had gone home, the last person left in the stadium that had anything to do with speedway was a cleaner. He had been a raker at the track in the 1950s. The rakers were a strong, hard-working group who had the most physically exhausting job in speedway. The sand that was thrown to the outside of the track by the riders' back wheels had to be pulled in towards the white line. As much as possible had to be moved between races and the rakers had to work hard and fast. In addition to actually pulling the track level, it was the rakers' job to find the holes that might appear in the track and fill them up. A raker had to have a good idea of the most popular 'line' taken by the riders as they cornered, as it would be pointless pulling the sand back on to a part of the track which the riders very rarely used. They had to collaborate with the tractor driver, who would give the track surface a smooth finish. These people also marshalled the riders and doubled-up as pushers-off to give the competitors the start they needed. Occasionally, they would pick up the bikes after a crash.

At Custom House, the rakers' uniforms were like a cross between sailors out of a comic opera and Spanish Civil War soldiers. Their roll-neck jumpers were blue, red or white with a large five-point star in a contrasting colour emblazoned on the front. On their backs were the crossed hammers. Their heads were covered with a beret, which might have matched the jumper or the star, or depart from any kind of conformity of hue. Before the final raker left, he turned to look at the empty stadium one more time. He paused, then slipped through the great main gates and, without looking back, disappeared into the maze of streets that surrounded the arena. Not even ghosts watched. For the first time in the best part of half a century, the stadium was truly empty. Not a soul left. All spirit gone. Only memories flitted across the place where so many dreams were made and lost.

Work on the demolition of Custom House Stadium was not, in the end, started until October. As such the Bombers could have finished their season. The bulldozers moved in at the end of 1972. The death of an era was marked by gangs of workmen tearing down a part of speedway, sporting and East London history. The famous old arena had, in its time, given immeasurable pleasure to so many people of all ages, over generations of families. It was all gone by 1973. Within a few years, the whole site was covered by the housing estate that now occupies the space where the stadium once stood. The estate has a Croombs, a Wilkinson and a Young Road. It has a Hoskins, an Atkinson and a Lawson Close – greatly loved and timeless names that would be honoured at least for a few more years as the West Ham Speedway Supporters' Club, the spirit of East London speedway, was to carry on long after the team and the oval it contested had disappeared. From silver sand to greensward: the first bend of the West Ham track was, by the mid-1970s, just a small green patch at the back of Wilkinson Road.

As a track died in the docklands of London, so one was opening at Cost Mesa in California, where speedway was being reintroduced to North America in a sustained manner. A number of British League riders were to race there, and, during the early 1970s, more tracks were opened, mainly in California. At that time, plans were also afoot to take the sport to the holiday island of Majorca to entertain the developing tourist invasion from Britain.

East Germany was another communist country of the time that was a rapidly improving speedway force. It has produced riders good enough to appear in a World Championship Final. However, Scandinavia apart, Western Europe did not altogether take to speedway. At one time or another, most of its countries staged the sport and West Germany had been the venue for some big meetings, drawing good crowds. Austria and France produced a handful of meetings, and there was some interest in Italy. On the team front, Sweden, Poland, England, Australia, Denmark, New Zealand and the United States had, by the start of the 1970s, all occupied the number one spot on the world stage at some time.

By the early 1970s, the World Championship had qualifying rounds that were split up into zones – Great Britain, Scandinavia and the Continent. Each area ran a series of qualifying rounds, semi-finals, and finals to determine the final sixteen. In the final itself, each rider met every other opponent only once.

West Ham and its track may have been no more, but it left a legacy. For example, by the early 1970s, Dave Jessup had established himself as a favourite with the London crowds. He had been a Lion at Wembley before moving to another lions' den at Leicester in 1972. Here he became part of one of speedway's best one/two rider combinations of any team, with England captain Ray Wilson. Wilson was now a dedicated rider. He was the quiet, modest man of speedway, who, like Barry Briggs – the rider Wilson modelled himself on – neither drank nor smoked. He liked to take care of his own machines. He always had two bikes with him at meetings. His Jawa machines, like his leathers and boots, glistened as the result of constant polishing.

Wilson loved to watch other forms of motorcycle sport, especially road racing and scrambling. A hard, forceful rider, many thought Ray would one day become a World Champion. It was also in 1972 that Jessup made his first impact in the World Championship. He reached the British Final, however, he failed to qualify for his first World Final, scoring only 7 points, but he was on his way.

CONCLUSION

The Pit Marshal

A most important fellow this, for in his hands lies the smooth running of the meeting. He will work under the direction of the Clerk of the Course whom I will speak about in a moment, but he is responsible for the general organisation within the Pit area, and for seeing that riders are warned of the imminence of their races so that they are prepared to go out onto the track with the least possible delay between heats. He will first check that all the riders scheduled and programmed to take part in the meeting are present, and he will report any absentees to the Clerk of the Course and to the Referee. He will see that the Colour Marshal is present and properly equipped, that the man in charge of fuel is in position, and that the 'Pushers' are all in attendance. In individual events he will be the man who deals with the choice of starting positions, usually with the use of a box specially designed for the purpose which, after a quick shake up, will allow balls coloured to correspond with the riders' helmet colours fall into slots numbered to indicate the starting positions. He will see that the pit gate is properly fastened in position so that no silly accidents can take place. Before the meeting he has the task of getting the official forms signed first by the captain of each team, verifying that all the riders have received their pay for previous meetings, and secondly by the Clerk of the Course to verify that all the necessary equipment etc. is in order, and thirdly by each team manager to verify that all the riders are properly equipped and so on. These forms are then given by the Pit Marshal to the Referee. This is a job for the 'Sergeant Major' type, who can issue swift and strict instructions and who can deal with those riders – that appear in almost every team – who seem to be keener to sit on their fuel cans in the Pits than they are to go out and race.

Silver, L. 'The Vital Cogs' in *The Speedway Annual* compiled by Silver, L. and Douglas, P. (London, Pelham Books, 1969)

On the afternoon of Saturday 28 July 1928, 40,000 had turned out to watch Sprouts Elder, Art Pechar, Ivor Creek and others practise the new sporting rage. On Tuesday 12 October 1971, barely 3,000 saw the Hammers beaten by local rivals Hackney in the London Cup. The summer and winter of East London speedway might thus be encapsulated. On that cold night, West Ham chief Gordon Parkins commented:

I can only say that if the stadium is still here for 1972 then the Hammers will be racing! We all know that there are many rumours about the sale and redevelopment of the stadium, and many tears would be shed if the day really came to pass and the bulldozers moved in.

The West Ham Balance Sheet

Johnnie Hoskins, during his time at Custom House before the Second World War, and Arthur Atkinson, one of his successors in the mid-1940s, regularly used to speak of the Custom House 'forty thou' – 40,000 being the average attendance that they expected for Tuesday night home matches. This was a time when West Ham speedway support humbled that attracted by West Ham United Football Club. Speedway's economic structure – the profits to promoters and rewards to the riders – corresponded to the clicks of the turnstiles. However, by the early 1970s, an average gate of 4,000 was considered good at most venues and, in the last years of West Ham speedway, it was not competing with its illustrious soccer neighbour, as a comparison between the respective profits after tax of the two concerns reveals;

Year	West Ham United Football Co. Ltd.	West Ham Speedway Ltd.
1968	£13,775	£2,567
1969	£52,675	£1,907
1970	£31,438	£789

The returns for the football club are in respect of years ending 31 July; those for the speedway company cover years ending 31 March.

There is a similar dramatic comparison between gross figures that actually changed hands at the turnstiles at the Upton Park and Custom House, both grounds of top division clubs in their respective sports. West Ham United received £252,696 from paying customers during 1970, compared with £22,866 from speedway crowds. This is a source of the discrepancy between the profits of the two organisations.

That £22,866 was West Ham Speedway's principal income for 1970. Other sources of revenue were programme sales (this amounted to £3,505), £1,679 from events staged on a pooled basis by the BSPA, £562 'commission' on a meeting staged on behalf of the BSPA and £236 from their supporters' club. Out of this came the £10,811 paid for starts, points and trophies over 31 meetings held at Custom House in a season. Commission to West Ham Stadium company by way of rent cost £2,716. Advertising and publicity accounted for £1,178. The only other four-figure sum in the accounts was £1,347, which was spent on the management and promotion of the team. So, West Ham Speedway's actual profit, after tax, for the year was just the £789. As a member of the board once commented: 'If we promoted speedway for the sake of merely making money, we would be better off running a barber's shop!'

The Spirit Of The Tracks

Just after the Second World War, it seemed as though speedway might become the new summer sport in Britain. County cricket treasurers looked in awe and envy at the spectacle of 60,000 fans attending a National League match at Wembley in midweek. A crowd of cup final proportions watched the World Championships. Supporters' clubs,

Veteran Speedway Riders' Association dinner dance in the early 1970s. From left to right, back row: Ron Howse, Wally Green, Jean Baker (West Ham office secretary), Reg Fearman and Howdy Byford. Front row: Pat Clarke, Colin Clarke and Jack Cooley.

their colourful pennants fluttering in the man-made breeze of motorcycle exhaust, cheered on their heroes with energy, excitement and delight. The National League grew to two and then three divisions. What attracted many was the honest conflict of the sport. It is the most satisfying of ironies that a mechanistic sport should have the vivid visual impact of medieval chivalry and courage. No other sport evokes more strongly than speedway the mindscape of Arthurian legend or the spirit of knightly joust. The rider pulls on his goggles and gauntlets as the combatants of old donned their armour. His colours stand out against the crowd and the sky. He has his devoted squires making last-second adjustments to his mount.

And yet, for all this, this latter-day George lost his fight with the dragon of television. It is about fifty years now since the speedway crowds began to melt away. Attempts to put National League matches on the television screen proved unsuccessful, largely because cameramen tended to focus on the leading rider and often ignored the other three. An official from the Speedway Control Board once commented that he had seen speedway decline steadily since the rise of television. Rather optimistically, he argued: 'That means that if there should happen to be a decline in television, there would very likely be a rise again of speedway. Perhaps there's the beginning of a feeling that, after years, the public is becoming disenchanted with TV.'

Certainly the Control Board was delighted when, in the early 1960s, West Ham Stadium drew nearly 15,000 spectators when it reopened for speedway, but when the TV theory was put to Jack McGregor in the mid-1960s, the veteran of the Belle Vue side scoffed at the idea: 'The boom came because after the war people were hungry for any entertainment they could get. The falling away was a natural reaction.'

The administrators of speedway were always persistent in their efforts to take a grip on the British sporting imagination. However, a neophyte to speedway in the mid-1960s would have doubted its ability to endure, as it looked as though whichever rider managed to scramble into the lead at the first bend was the odds-on favourite to win. Overtaking in the straight was far less common than was once the case; the art of cornering seemed to be the most crucial element of a rider's repertoire. This was not always the case, but that was how it often appeared, and for any sport to succeed on a mass scale, feats of skill against a background of chance must not only be done, they must be seen to be done.

However, to condemn speedway for not being something it wasn't may be doing it an aesthetic injustice. In Britain, soccer and cricket rule the sporting waves, and that is why a significant growth in speedway spectatorship would, by the early 1970s, have demanded a change in the psychological make-up of the average person, to whom a motorcycle engine was not quite synonymous with athletic prowess. That is why, by the start of the 1970s, the giants of the dirt track in Britain so rarely managed to impose their presence on the masses. Like jazz musicians and physicists, they remained celebrities only to each other and their loyal fans.

The sport does have a future, however, thanks, ironically, to television. Satellite TV is now creating a new, maybe larger than ever, worldwide audience for the speedway, using the modern Grand Prix format as a flagship. This, in turn, has generated a renewed interest in the sport's history and, in the process, has brought the wonderful names and characters contained in these pages back to life. Television, which was once seen as nemesis of speedway, could well be the saviour of the sport.

Looking back to the high days of speedway may teach us the lesson that to everything there is a season. There was once a saying in speedway that the part of the mechanics of the bike that made the difference was the 'nut' holding the handlebars. It was this that made the early days of sport its golden time. The machines at this time did not compensate for the shortcomings or depreciate the skills of the rider. The days when men rode against each other in a form of mechanised joust may be gone, and have taken their place in the past like those when knights won their spurs. But we have much to learn from their time and performances. They gave the world something that has never been replaced, a sense of daring – 'dash', as it was often called in the golden days of the track – exhibited in front of tens of thousands. It exemplified a spirit of adventure, of pushing the limits of man against man, machine against machine and perhaps the final confrontation, man against machine – which machines seem to have won, taking the spirit of speedway to themselves and thus ending the spectacle.

Harringay v. *West Ham, 1950. From left to right: Arthur Bush, Nobby Stock, Reg Fearman, with Howdy Byford bringing up the rear.*

Our matches now are ended
These our riders
As I foretold you, were all Hammers and
Are melted into exhaust, into heady fumes:
And, like the baseless fabric of television,
The twin towers, the gorgeous tracks,
The solemn SCB, the great Custom House Stadium itself,
Yes, all which it inherit shall dissolve,
And like the insubstantial West Ham fade,
Leave not a helmet behind. We are such stuff,
As dreams are made on, and our little life
Is rounded in an oval.

APPENDIX I: CHRONOLOGY

Specialist Lighting
There are certain statutory lights which have to be used at all Speedway tracks in England. First, there are the red warning lights which must be six in number. These can be switched on by the referee if he needs to stop a race in the interests of safety. They must be at a height of not more than 5 feet from the ground and situated so that they can be easily seen by the riders. In addition there are two green lights, one in the front of the starting gate positioned by the safety fence, and one behind the starting line (also by the safety fence). These are put on to indicate to the riders and to the starting marshal that they are under 'Starters orders. When the riders see this light go on whilst they are sitting at the tapes they rev their engines ready for the 'off'. In front of the starting gate at a distance of about 20-30 yards and at a height of about 10 feet, there is situated a bar on which are hung lights coloured to correspond with the riders' helmet covers. These are switched on by the referee to indicate that a rider has been excluded, i.e., if the rider with the red helmet cover has committed some misde-meanor then the red light is switched on and at the same time as this happens the starting marshal indicates to the rider that he is excluded by showing the red exclusion disk and the black flag simultaneously. The most recent addition to the specialist electrical equipment is the 'Dispute Box'. This is not obligatory; its use is merely for the information of the public to let them know that there is a hold-up between races because of a dispute with the referee or perhaps between Team Managers over some interpretation of the regulations. It is, as its name sug-gests, a box illuminated on the inside and with the words 'DISPUTE' cut out in the side of the box so that the public can see it easily. It is switched on by the referee as required. As an alternative to this box the referee may use the red warning lights instead.

Silver, L. 'Anatomy of a Speedway' in *The Speedway Annual* compiled by Silver, L. and Douglas, P. (London, Pelham Books, 1969)

West Ham Speedway

Address: Custom House Stadium, Prince Regent Lane, London
Years of Operation: *1928* Open; *1929-31* Southern League; *1932-33* National League; *1934* National League and Reserve League; *1935-37* National League; *1938-39* National League Division One; *1940-42* Open; *1946* National League; *1947-55* National League Division One; *1964* National League; *1965-67* British League; *1968-71* British League Division One; *1972* British Leasue Division Two
First meeting: 28 July 1928 **Track length**: 440 yards (1928-53); 413 yards (1954-72)
Nickname: Hammers (1930-71); Bombers (1972)
League Champions: 1937, 1963 **ACU Cup Winners**: 1938 **KO Cup Winners**: 1963

1928 Dirt Track Speedways Ltd stage the first meetings at West Ham. These are the pre-league days. Programmes comprise individual events and track record attempts.

1929 West Ham contest British speedway's first team competition, the Southern League.

1933 Victor Martin, Fred Fearnley and Stanley Greening take over management. West Ham stadium stages its first Test match: a crowd of 82,400 see England beat Australia.

1935 Johnnie Hoskins, the man who started speedway in Australia twelve years previously, moves in as manager. The sport's master showman, he introduces elephant parades, Russian dancers and children's hoop races in supporting roles to speedway.

1936 West Ham are bottom of the National League. Hoskins supplies supporters' club members – over 10,000 of them – with miniature wooden spoons to attach to their badges. The concept is a huge success (he could even market failure!).

1937 Hammers bounce back. Skippered by Tiger Stevenson – the team's captain for ten years in all – they are National League First Division Champions.

1938 Australian ace Bluey Wilkinson is West Ham's first World Champion.

1939 Hammers again have the favourite for the world crown in British bred Arthur Atkinson, but the war prevents the final taking place.

1946 Atkinson is now co-manager with Stan Greatrex. The team again finish bottom of the League.

1947 In May, Australian phenomenon Aub Lawson joins West Ham

1949 West Ham take fourth place in the League and reach the finals of both the National Trophy and the Knockout Cup.

1950 Johnnie Hoskins is back as promoter on behalf of businessman Alan Sanderson. Atkinson resumes riding career. Ken Brett becomes team manager. Wally Green joins West Ham's roll of world championship honour by finishing third. In August, Aub Lawson takes the Match Race title from Jack Parker.

1951 Lawson wins London Riders' Championship. West Ham finish fourth in the League.

1952 West Ham sign reigning world champion Jack Young from Edinburgh. The fee is a record £3,750. The Australian star takes the Match Race title from Ronnie Moore and keeps the world crown as a West Ham rider. The Hammers again finish fourth in the League.

1953 Hoskins goes to Belle Vue. Charles Ochiltree takes over West Ham. Tiger Stevenson is back with the Hammers as clerk of the course, later to be Ken Brett's successor as team manager. Jack Young tops the League averages and successfully defends his Match Race title against Freddie Williams and Split Waterman (he finally gave up the title undefeated). Young also takes London Riders' Championship. West Ham finish sixth in the League and although they reach the London Cup final are beaten by Harringay.

1954 Young lodges transfer request. He believes West Ham's 440-yard track is too big. The management duly reduces it to 415 yards. Young agrees to stay and retains the London Riders' Championship. West Ham finish in fifth place in the League.

1955 After struggling throughout the season, both in terms of winning matches and attracting the fans, and although Jack Young is top scorer in the League, West Ham finish as bottom club and suspend operations for the next eight years during the period of speedway's temporary decline.

1964 The National League, down to six tracks, needs a seventh to remain viable. A consortium of promoters, headed by Charles Ochiltree, re-open West Ham. There's a 15,000 crowd for the first meeting. Managed by ex-world champion Tommy Price, skippered by world champion yet-to-be Bjorn Knutsson, the team finish bottom of the League, but are beaten finalists in the last National Trophy competition to be staged.

1965 The new British League is launched. Hammers are inaugural champions – they are also Knockout Cup and London Cup winners. Captained by Scotland's Ken McKinlay, the team enjoy their most successful season ever. McKinlay wins the Brandonapolis and the Silver Sash from Jim Lightfoot. Sverre Harrfeldt wins the London Riders' Championship.

1966 Tommy Price resigns on the eve of the season. New chief Dave Lanning steers the team to the Knockout Cup final. Norwegian and Custom House idol Sverre Harrfeldt is second in the World Final. West Ham are seventh in the League but retain the London Cup. Norman Hunter is London Riders' Champion and third in the British Riders' Championship.

1967 Although the Hammers take third place in the League, get to the final of the Knockout Cup and hold on to the London Cup for the third successive year, it is the beginning of the end of West Ham Stadium. A third of the spectator accommodation is demolished and the land sold.

1968 West Ham take sixth spot in the League.

1969 West Ham finish second from bottom in the League.

1970 Dave Lanning resigns. West Ham appoint their last controller, former Norwich chief, Gordon Parkins. Speedway's greatest disaster occurs when a party of West Ham riders visiting the Continent are involved in a road accident in Belgium. Those who die include team manager Phil Bishop (a pre-war rider), Peter Bradshaw and Martyn Piddock – two immensely promising young prospects.

1971 West Ham race their final season. They finish bottom of the League. In December, the promoting company announce they have sold out to Second Division Ipswich.

1972 Neighbouring promotion Romford – who are themselves without a track – live in hope that they might use West Ham's facilities until such a time as the developers move in, and they find a new home of their own. The West Ham riders are re-allocated to rival promotions.

West Ham Top Twenty

Who was the top speedway Hammer of all time? An informal poll of older followers of the team, carried out by *Speedway '72* magazine in 1972, suggested there was little to choose between Bluey Wilkinson, undisputed king of the pre-war era, and fellow Australian Jack Young, the Custom House top man of the 1950s.

1=	Bluey Wilkinson	10	Christer Lofqvist
1=	Jack Young	11	Wally Green
3	Tiger Stevenson	12	Malcolm Craven
4	Bjorn Knutsson	13	Gerry Hussey
5	Arthur Atkinson	14	Norman Hunter
6	Sverre Harrfeldt	15	Colin Watson
7	Eric Chitty	16	Jimmy Gibb
8	Aub Lawson	17	Bob Harrison
9	Ken McKinlay	18	Charlie Spinks

Riders who died in racing accidents on the Custom House track

Ernie Roccio (Wimbledon)
Harry Eyre (local novice)
Teo Teodorowicz (Swindon)
Dave Wills (West Ham)

APPENDIX II: STATISTICS

The Public Address System

Naturally every stadium needs some form of public address system for without it no member of the public would be able to be kept in touch with the essential information necessary for him or her to enjoy the meeting. These are the basic essentials of a speedway track and added to them of course, must be such things as turnstiles, toilets, snack bars and so on, as well as car parking facilities and track overhead lighting so that meetings can be held after dark ... a promoter needs certain other equipment in order to carry on his business. He needs, for example, a tractor fitted with a removable blade and an angle-iron grader for use in track preparation and maintenance. He also needs certain other paraphernalia such as race flags, exclusion discs, track hand rakes, staff uniforms, water hoses or watercart and a hundred and one other items far too numerous to mention here. The cost of providing all this equipment for you to enjoy your Speedway can run into many thousand of pounds, so you can imagine the promoter's feelings when, after providing all this equipment, the rain comes down and the public stop at home. However, his rewards when the public use the facilities he gives them to their fullest can be enough to make him a very happy man!

Silver, L. 'Anatomy of a Speedway' in *The Speedway Annual* compiled by Silver, L. and Douglas, P. (London, Pelham Books, 1969)

Star Riders' Championship

1932	1st	Eric Langton *(England & Belle Vue)*
	2nd	Vic Huxley *(Australia & Wimbledon)*
	3rd	Dick Case *(Australia & Wimbledon)*
1933	1st	Tom Farndon *(England & Crystal Palace)*
	2nd	Ron Johnson *(Australia & Crystal Palace)*
	3rd	Bluey Wilkinson *(Australia & West Ham)*
1934	1st	Jack Parker *(England & Harringay)*
	2nd	Eric Langton *(England & Belle Vue)*
	3rd	Ginger Lees *(England & Wembley)*
1935	1st	Frank Charles *(England & Wembley)*
	2nd	Jack Ormston *(England & Harringay)*
	3rd	Max Grosskreutz *(Australia & Belle Vue)*

Sunday Dispatch British Riders' Championship (Venue: Wembley)

1946	*1st*	Tommy Price *(England & Wembley)*	15 points
	2nd	Bill Kitchen *(England & Wembley)*	13 points
	3rd	Jack Parker *(England & Belle Vue)*	12 points
1947	*1st*	Jack Parker *(England & Belle Vue)*	14 points
	2nd	Bill Kitchen *(England & Wembley)*	14 points
	3rd	Bill Longley *(Australia & New Cross)*	11 points
1948	*1st*	Vic Duggan *(Australia & Harringay)*	14 points
	2nd	Ron Johnson *(Australia & New Cross)*	13 points
	3rd	Alec Statham *(England & Wimbledon)*	13 points

British League Speedway Champions (to 1972)

Division One

1965	West Ham
1966	Halifax
1967	Swindon
1968	Coventry
1969	Poole
1970	Belle Vue
1971	Belle Vue
1972	Belle Vue

Division Two

1968	Belle Vue
1969	Belle Vue
1970	Canterbury
1971	Eastbourne
1972	Crewe

Club success in London Riders' Championship (1930-72)

Wimbledon	7
New Cross (Crystal Palace)	7
West Ham	6
Hackney	4
Wembley	3
Swindon/Harringay/Unattached	1

London Riders' Championship (1930-72)

Rider (team)	Year	Venue
Jack Ormston (Wembley)	1930	Crystal Palace
Joe Francis (Crystal Palace)	1931	Crystal Palace
Not held	*1932-33*	*New Cross*
Tom Farndon (New Cross)	1934	New Cross
Tom Farndon (New Cross)	1935	New Cross
Vic Huxley (Wimbledon)	1936	New Cross
Jack Milne (New Cross)	1937	New Cross
Eric Chitty (West Ham)	1938	New Cross
Jack Milne (New Cross)	1939	New Cross
Not held	*1940-44*	
Ron Johnson (unattached)	1945	New Cross
Ron Johnson (New Cross)	1946	New Cross
Vic Duggan (Harringay)	1947	New Cross
Split Waterman (Wembley)	1948	New Cross
Alec Statham (Wimbledon)	1949	New Cross
Cyril Roger (New Cross)	1950	New Cross
Aub Lawson (West Ham	1951	New Cross
Ronnie Moore (Wimbledon)	1952	New Cross
Jack Young (West Ham)	1953	Harringay
Jack Young (West Ham)	1954	West Ham
Barry Briggs (Wimbledon)	1955	Wimbledon
Brian Crutcher(Wembley)	1956	Wembley
Not held	*1957-62*	
Norman Hunter (Hackney)	1963	Hackney
Mike Broadbanks (Swindon)	1964	West Ham
Sverre Harrfeldt (West Ham)	1965	Hackney
Norman Hunter (West Ham)	1966	Hackney
Colin Pratt (Hackney)	1967	Hackney
Colin Pratt (Hackney)	1968	Hackney
Trevor Hedge (Wimbledon)	1969	Hackney
Trevor Hedge(Wimbledon)	1970	Hackney
Bengt Jansson(Hackney)	1971	Hackney
Ronnie Moore(Wimbledon)	1972	Hackney

World Speedway Championship (1936-72)

Year	Venue	1st	2nd	3rd
1936	Wembley	Van Praag *(Aus)*	E. Langton *(Eng)*	B. Wilkinson *(Aus)*
1937	Wembley	J. Milne *(USA)*	W. Lamoreaux *(USA)*	C. Milne *(USA)*
1938	Wembley	B. Wilkinson *(Aus)*	J. Milne *(USA)*	W. Lamoreaux *(USA)*
1939-1948		No competition		
1949	Wembley	T. Price *(Eng)*	J. Parker *(Eng)*	L. Lawson *(Eng)*
1950	Wembley	F. Williams *(Wales)*	W. Green *(Eng)*	G. Warren *(Aus)*
1951	Wembley	J. Young *(Aus)*	S. Waterman *(Eng)*	J. Biggs *(Aus)*
1952	Wembley	J. Young *(Aus)*	F. Williams *(Wales)*	B. Oakley *(Eng)*
1953	Wembley	F. Williams *(Wales)*	S. Waterman *(Eng)*	G. Mardon *(NZ)*
1954	Wembley	R. Moore *(NZ)*	B. Crutcher *(Eng)*	O. Nygen (Swe)
1955	Wembley	P. Craven *(Eng)*	R. Moore *(NZ)*	B. Briggs *(NZ)*
1956	Wembley	O. Fundin *(Swe)*	R. Moore *(NZ)*	A. Forrest *(Eng)*
1957	Wembley	B. Briggs *(NZ)*	O. Fundin *(Swe)*	P. Craven *(Eng)*
1958	Wembley	B. Briggs *(NZ)*	O. Fundin *(Swe)*	A. Lawson *(Aus)*
1959	Wembley	R. Moore *(NZ)*	O. Fundin *(Swe)*	B. Briggs *(NZ)*
1960	Wembley	O. Fundin *(Swe)*	R. Moore *(NZ)*	P. Craven *(Eng)*
1961	Mälmo	O. Fundin *(Swe)*	B. Knutsson *(Swe)*	G. Nordin *(Swe)*
1962	Wembley	P. Craven *(Eng)*	B. Briggs *(Eng)*	O. Fundin *(Swe)*
1963	Wembley	O. Fundin *(Swe)*	B. Knutsson *(Swe)*	B. Briggs *(NZ)*
1964	Gothenburg	B. Briggs *(NZ)*	L. Plechanov (USSR)	O. Fundin *(Swe)*
1965	Wembley	B. Knutsson *(Swe)*	L. Plechanov (USSR)	O. Fundin *(Swe)*
1966	Gothenburg	B. Briggs *(NZ)*	S. Harrfeldt *(Nor)*	A. Woryna *(Pol)*
1967	Wembley	O. Fundin *(Swe)*	B. Jansson *(Swe)*	I. Mauger *(NZ)*
1968	Gothenburg	I. Mauger *(NZ)*	B. Briggs *(NZ)*	E. Jancarz *(Pol)*
1969	Wembley	I. Mauger *(NZ)*	B. Briggs *(NZ)*	S. Sjosten *(Swe)*
1970	Wroclaw	I. Mauger *(NZ)*	P. Walsozek *(Pol)*	A. Woryna *(Pol)*
1971	Gothenburg	Ole Oksen *(Den)*	Ivan Mauger *(NZ)*	Bengt Jansson *(Swe)*

Leading Speedway Nations
(Based on World Team Cup points up to and including 1970)

Nation	Points
Sweden	353
Britain (England)	266
Poland	244
USSR	100
Czech	80

World Championship Merit Table (to 1970)

Table of leading World Championship final riders with a minimum of five appearances. The average is obtained by dividing the number of appearances into the points scored.

Rider	Country	Appearances	Points	Average
Ivan Mauger	New Zealand	5	68	13.6
Barry Briggs	New Zealand	17	200	11.76
Ove Fundin	Sweden	15	173	11.53
Olle Nygen	Sweden	5	54	10.8
Ronnie Moore	New Zealand	13	139	10.69
Bjorn Knuttsson	Sweden	6	64	10.66
Jack Young	Australia	7	70	10
Peter Craven	England	10	96	9.6
Jack Parker	England	5	48	9.6
Split Waterman	England	5	48	9.6
Igor Plechanov	USSR	6	56	9.33
Brian Crutcher	England	6	54	9
Antoni Woryna	Poland	5	42	8.4
Aub Lawson	Australia	9	73	8.11
Arthur Forrest	England	5	37	7.4
Ken McKinlay	Scotland	9	66	7.33
Peter Moore	Australia	5	34	6.8
Rune Sormander	Sweden	7	45	6.42
Ron How	England	8	47	5.87
Nigel Boocock	England	6	35	5.38
Mike Broadbanks	England	5	19	3.8
Andrzei Wyglenda	Poland	5	17	3.4

World Team Cup (to 1970)

Year	Venue	1st (points)	2nd (points)	3rd (points)	4th (points)
1960	Gothenburg	Sweden (44)	England (32)	Czech (15)	Poland (7)
1961	Wroclaw	Poland (32)	Sweden (31)	England (21)	Czech (12)
1962	Slany	Sweden (36)	Britain (24)	Poland (20)	Czech (16)
1963	Vienna	Sweden (37)	Czech (27)	Britain (25)	Poland (7)
1964	Abensberg	Sweden (34)	USSR (25)	Britain (21)	Poland (16)
1965	Kempten	Poland (38)	Sweden (33)	Britain (18)	USSR (7)
1966	Wroclaw	Poland (40)	USSR (26)	Sweden (22)	Britain (8)
1967	Mälmo	Sweden (32)	Poland (26)	Britain/USSR (19)	
1968	Wembley	Britain (40)	Sweden (30)	Poland (19)	Czech (7)
1969	Rybnik	Poland (31)	Britain (27)	USSR (23)	Sweden (12)
1970	Wembley	Sweden (42)	Britain (31)	Poland (20)	Czech (3)